LEADING RESILIENCE

Strategies for Thriving in Disruptive Times

Eltigani Ahmed, Ph.D

ISBN—Online: 978-9914-49-830-1
ISBN—Paperback: 978-9914-49-831-8

First Edition: 2023

Copyediting by Wandering Words (www.wanderingwordsmedia.com)
First Proofreading by Wandering Words (www.wanderingwordsmedia.com)
Second Proofreading by Lead Entrepreneurs Network School (informlens@gmail.com)
Layout and Formatting by Formatted Books (https://formattedbooks.com)
Covers Design by 100-Covers (www.100covers.com)
Content Indexing by Weaver Indexing (www.weaverindexing.com)

Printed in the United States of America

DEDICATION

To my family:

Tamador, Arwa, Areej, Aiman, Muhannad, Mohamed
You are a bond of my form. I devote the word to You.
You are my anchor in storm. I pledge my love to You.

CONTENTS

LIST OF TABLES

PREFACE

Why do disruptive events affect homogeneous-ecosystem organizations variably? Why do seemingly robust organizations fail without forewarning? Why do some organizations capitalize and grow in disruptive times? What makes some organizations more efficient in value creation from comparable resources? What makes small organizations more agile? Why does a change in leadership result in mixed fortunes? What makes organizations fail? What makes them succeed?

These questions set me on the curious path of an unpredicted expedition, and my quest for answers drove me along two lanes: a solitary journey to my doctorate research and an enjoyable sail to this book. My twin pathways converged onto one destination: resilience. Kelly Morgan wrote, "Changes are inevitable and not always controllable. We can only control how we manage, react to, and work through the change process." When organizations face disruptions, resilience becomes a differentiating factor.

Building resilience is synonymous with putting on a seatbelt in a moving vehicle—it is unnoticed on a routine drive but a lifesaver in an accident. Resilience preparedness is tantamount to the insurance premiums we pay to recover our assets in a loss. We do not wait for the loss to pay our premiums. Likewise, we may not have to wait for a disruption to prepare our organizations. Resilience is an acquirable trait initiated through leadership resolve, nurtured through technology, cemented through process enhancement, scaled up through employee training, and transferred to generations through stakeholder buy-in.

Resilient organizations are genuinely agile. They know how to protect their strengths, capitalize on opportunities, grow from weaknesses, and triumph over threats. They adjust operations and reallocate resources for sustained growth. "Resilience" is a notch beyond "performance." Performing organizations are not necessarily resilient, but resilient organizations are performant on average. Resilience transcends financial performance to structural sturdiness, ethical prowess, cultural sanity, and socioeconomic intelligence.

Organizations intentionally cultivate resilience, and resilience sustains organizations. Organizations and resilience are like trees and water. Trees help make rain through transpiration and photosynthesis, where moisture originating from roots gathers on leaves and evaporates into the atmosphere to condense into clouds and pour back to Mother Earth to sustain trees and other life. In the same way, organizations create resilience, and resilience sustains organizations. It is like a payback from a long-term investment. Resilience is a long-term process that pays back for years ahead.

Organizational resilience is a novel concept that only recently migrated from behavioral psychology with hitherto meager practical applications that have primarily been limited to developed economies. There is still no consensus on the definition, conceptualization, operationalization, and measurement of resilience. Furthermore, modeling resilience around crisis has not been adequately explored until now, presenting good scholarship pastures for researchers aiming to dig more into this area of scholarship.

This book reflects on the concept of resilience with fresh lenses from the perspective of volatile markets. It adopts a beginner method to popularize the concept of resilience and bring it out of the abstract academic discourse. The reader will encounter various anecdotes, stories, and practical cases demonstrating how resilience works in organizations and individuals.

Leading Resilience – Strategies for Thriving in Disruptive Times is a pioneering attempt to demystify and propagate the concept of resilience into organizational space. In this book, I explore the importance of resilience and discuss strategies organizations can use to propagate resilience. I study some cases of organizations that have successfully used resilience to their advantage in various geographical contexts worldwide. The book is one of the first attempts to model resilience in a dynamic crisis context and propose desirable traits of resilient organizations at each stage of crisis manifestation: pre-crisis (crisis head), within-crisis (crisis body), and post-crisis (crisis tail). The central argument in this book is that being resilient at each crisis segment is conditional upon being resilient at the adjacent segment(s). Perhaps most interestingly, tools, investments, capabilities, and knowledge developed in one crisis segment are not necessarily relevant in the adjacent segment(s). This argument has profound implications for resource management, asset turnover, human resource policies, investments in technology, and strategic planning.

The book interrogates the root causes of why strategic and transitional plans fail to bring about lasting organizational transformation. Accordingly, the book integrates the utility of resilience resources and advances resilience capability leadership to orchestrate organizational resources as a potential differentiating factor in organizational resilience development and maintenance.

We live in unprecedented, disruptive times characterized by blurring boundaries, cutting-edge technologies, globally integrated markets, and the increased frequency of natural disasters and political unrest. Our modern lifestyle is loaded with competing priorities, and we have insufficient amounts of our most priceless asset—time. Cognizant of this fact, I migrated from the traditional method of book presentation. I open book chapters with stories to spice up your reading experience. Throughout the book, you will read the New Choluteca Bridge story, the Chelyabinsk meteor analogy, Ninja Rat adventures, Sir Richard Branson's daring journey, Captain Chesley Sullenberger's stubbornness on the River Hudson, Titanic's calamity, the Honey Badger's resiliency, and Horatio Gates Spafford's remembrance. These stories connote deep metaphors to stimulate readers' intellectual curiosity as they provide a profound reflection on the corresponding chapters.

In this book, I apply an exploratory approach by first tracing crisis happenstances to lay a launching pad for developing resilience manifestations. I then discuss the desirable resilience traits at each crisis happenstance with practical cases of resilient and non-resilient organizations. I analyze leadership actions and strategies for attaining and maintaining resilience. I then discuss resilience in small and medium-sized enterprises (SMEs) and nonprofit sectors to present a thorough overview of resilience manifestations. I end the book by proposing a practical Leading Resilience Index containing 10 scales, 35 dimensions, and 165 Likert-scale items. The seed variables and constructs that form the basis of the Leading Resilience Index (LRI) are pilot tested; therefore, the LRI can be adopted with minimal adjustments to assess organizations' resilience preparedness. The proposed LRI contains detailed instructions on how the index can be administered, scored, interpreted, and reported.

Most chapters of the book begin with a section titled "Springboard" and end with "Self-cascading Reflections" and "Bend your Mind." "Springboard" is an epigraphic idiom summarising the highest moment of the chapter. "Self-cascading Reflections" summarize thoughts and lessons from the chapter. "Bend your Mind" presents ideas indirectly inspired by the chapter's content and aims to leave the reader with a lingering taste from the preceding chapter and an appetizer to the subsequent chapter. The book presents new concepts in organizational leadership discourse, such as Adversity-Practical-Social-Emotional-Spiritual Intelligence cores (APSES), Crisis-Induced Growth Realization Opportunities (CIGRO), Crisis-Induced Profit-Making Opportunities (CIPMO), and Management-Strategy-Emergency-Resilience (MASTER).

This book is a companion to leaders and executives—from startups to large corporations—seeking to build resiliency by providing them with the tools they need to create a culture of resilience and manage resources in times of disruption. I present this book to government officials, nonprofit organizations, and other stakeholders looking to develop a more resilient society. I offer this book to anyone in business, technology, or public policy interested in preparing organizations for the future. I hand this book to academics and researchers interested in garnering a broader understanding of resilience.

I hope this book will contribute to knowledge, satisfy your quest for an enjoyable read, and answer some questions and concerns about leading resilience in disruptive times.

INTRODUCTION

On a September morning of 2001, a cruising civilian aircraft abruptly chuted without forewarning as a premeditated assault in the cockpit unfolded, with more horrific scenes momentarily stretching into New York and Virginia.[1] This was not a Hollywood movie but a reality, in all senses of the word. A second aircraft exploded moments after in Pennsylvania, killing all passengers on board.[1] The September 11 terrorist attack on US soil made a lasting impact on the global security order; in addition, it caused the destruction of the iconic World Trade Center, the deaths of thousands of innocent civilians, the loss of over half a million jobs, the war in the Middle East, and a long-term effect on the world economy.[2]

In November 2002, a viral infection known as Severe Acute Respiratory Syndrome spread in several countries, leading to a paralysis of airline operations and overwhelming the health services in the affected countries. The 21st century's first deadly pandemic spread to 20 countries within one year, causing untold disruptions.[3]

In December 2004, a young man's life was instantaneously taken by a tsunami while enjoying a fresh-morning swim off the East African Watamu beach on the Indian

Ocean. The deceased young man joined over 200,000 people who lost their lives across 14 countries that morning. An earthquake had ripped the ocean bed apart over 2,485 miles (4,000 km) away and three miles (five kilometers) deep, causing a 100-meter-high, killer aquatic surge.[4] In the same year, another earthquake killed 100,000 people and left more than three million without homes across Asia.[5] One year later, in August 2005, Hurricane Katrina landed on New Orleans and its surroundings, killing more than 1300 people and causing economic damages estimated conservatively at around $125 billion.[6]

In 2008, systemic shocks triggered by the United States' housing subprime mortgages resulted in a prolonged, worldwide recession and a more devastating, second-round commodity shock, disturbing developing countries' economies. A fund manager in the US managed to close a credit default swap moments before the crisis and saved $60 million in what was seen as a strategic, risk-management move.[7] Two years later, in January 2010, Haiti experienced one of the strongest earthquakes since the 1800s, resulting in the death of more than 2000 people and over two billion dollars in economic loss.[8] Before the end of the global recession, a police officer in Tunis, the capital city of Tunisia, demeaned a fruit vendor in January 2011, causing the fruit vendor to set himself on fire. The death of the fruit vendor sparked region-wide protests that led to the downfall of several regimes in the Middle East and North Africa.[9]

Ebola Virus Disease was reported in March 2014 in West Africa, and within three months, it spread to seven countries, causing death and economic disruption.[10] In December 2019, the world hibernated due to the COVID-19 pandemic, caused by a highly-contagious virus first discovered in China. It spread to tens of countries, infecting over two million people and recording more than 100 thousand deaths within three months. By the end of 2022, COVID-19 fatalities reached 15 million in addition to an estimated cost of $13 billion to the world economy.[11]

In February 2020, a locust plague wreaked havoc in East Africa. Only weighing about two grams each, locusts can fly up to 93 miles (150 km) per day and become lethal in swarms, causing crop decimation and food crises.[12] Six months later, in August 2020, an ammonium-nitrate warehouse exploded in Beirut, killing 300 people and leaving 300,000 Beirutians without shelter.[13]

In February 2022, a geopolitical conflict and the prospects of a nuclear apocalypse rapidly escalated from the Russia-Ukraine conflict. Estimates put the global economic cost of the war at nearly one trillion dollars in less than one year.[14] The Russia-Ukraine conflict exposed millions to the greatest cost-of-living crisis in modern history, pushing some into abject poverty.[15]

The preceding world events demonstrate that the 21st century arrived with unprecedented disruptive episodes, tossing the world into chaos every two years or so and awakening organizations to the crystallization of cataclysm in stark reality. What do we take away from all this? We take that some crises are unavoidable and dissimilar. Therefore, each crisis requires unique forms of preparedness. We take that crises are continuously occurring, closely entangled, and mutually reinforcing. At each crisis happenstance, well-crafted business models suddenly ceased to make sense, and business executives rushed to the drawing board to resuscitate erstwhile cheerfully lauded strategies that, retrospectively, appeared to have been painted on moving sand. Most business strategists would not have predicted the level of the sand's motion.

One could then ask, why so much herd-style futurism if a single unpredicted event can undo all strategies and call for a new crisis-plan boot camp? Well, one would want to believe that the holy grail of a successful strategy is—and you may be shocked by this—a resilience strategy. Strategizing for resilience is tantamount to planning in that it is relevant no matter what. Resilience strategies are planned, executed, protected, and transferred through leadership strategies. Hence, the term "resilience leadership" is coined in this book to represent leadership actions geared toward developing and implementing resilience strategies. In this book, resilience leadership refers to resilience direction, resilience quality, resilience capability, resilience talent, resilience adequacy, and personal leadership intelligence.

While the recurrence and intensity of crises seem to have rekindled an interest in resilience, the concept of crisis that makes a testing pad for resilience has not received its fair share of scholarly attention. This book attempts to bridge the gap by presenting an orthodox assessment of crises in what they portend for organizations. In this book, I demystify resilience and advocate its propagation in modern organizations. Organizational resilience is an emergent concept borrowed from behavioral psychology and is used most of the time to refer to the structural robustness of organizations in the face of physical disasters, such as earthquakes and flooding. This book is an unguided walk in the wilderness of an exhumed concept as it attempts to broaden the construct of resilience from the traditional connotation of being solid in the face of natural disasters to the ability to thrive in the face of natural and human-made crises.

This book is divided into 10 chapters. The first three chapters deal with foundational elements of crisis and resilience. Chapter One unpacks the concept of crisis in its various forms and manifestations, including crisis manifestation as a symptom of an underlying disorder, as evidence of a progressive degeneration process, as a sign of issue management failure, as evidence of extreme hardship, as a symptom of an uncontrollable situation, as a manifestation of probability-impact spread, and as a value-creation opportunity. Chapter Two demystifies the concept of organizational resilience, including its manifestations as a contingency planning process, as a resilience strategy anchor, and as a sustainability management tool. Chapter Three introduces the resilience cycle and models resilience around crisis. It proposes desirable organizational traits for each crisis happenstance, including those at pre-crisis, within-crisis, and post-crisis stages.

The following three chapters deal with accelerating elements of resilience. Chapter Four discusses resilience resources, including financial, human, and reputational resource buffers. The buffers are available but untapped resources that an organization resorts to for accelerating its resilience momentum during disruptive shocks. They constitute reserve assets that can be tapped into when the need arises. Chapter Five expounds on how resilience resources can be brought to life through deliberate and concerted actions of resilience-resource orchestration. It discusses resilience-resource structuring, resilience-resource bundling, and resilience-resource leveraging. Chapter Six discusses resilience leadership. Resilience leadership provides an organizational compass by identifying resilience direction, measuring resilience quality, gauging resilience capability, assessing resilience talent, and determining resilience adequacy. The relevance of resilience leadership arises from the fact that the lack of a compass to navigate a stable path toward vision realization renders resource abundance useless. Chapter Six also presents elements of personal leadership intelligence cores and discusses adversity intelligence, practical intelligence, social intelligence, emotional intelligence, and spiritual intelligence. The personal leadership intelligence core is critical to ensuring an organization has the right leadership mindset to withstand adversity and lead resiliently.

The remaining four chapters of the book deal with practical elements of resilience. Chapter Seven analyzes worldwide cases of corporate success and failure to draw commonalities and answer the question why some corporations succeed while others fail. Chapters Eight and Nine discuss SME and nonprofit sector resilience, respectively. SME and nonprofit are peculiar in many respects. Despite their instrumental economic development and social cohesion roles, they figure less frequently in national policy priorities. This book brings SME and nonprofit resilience discussion to the fore. Chapter Ten presents the LRI. The index is structured in line with the book's content, containing 10 scales, 35 dimensions, and 165 Likert-scale items.

Apart from the opening and concluding chapters, each chapter begins with "Springboard" and ends with "Self-cascading Reflections" and "Bend your Mind." "Springboard" gives readers the impetus to dive into the chapter. "Self-cascading Reflection" and "Bend your Mind" offer a reflection on the chapter content. Finding and interpreting the connections are at the reader's discretion.

Lewis Carroll said, "If you do not know your destiny, any path becomes yours." Finding oneself in a crisis blows dual myopia into one's spirit: myopia arising from a loss of compass and myopia triggered by a blurred vision ahead. Engulfed in a moment of the darkness and wrecked in a sea of despair, the guts to figure out an anchor at the shores of life is the difference between survival and demise; hope and anguish; resilience and fragility; past and future; and prosperity and regression. Having the guts to see hope in despair is the essence of being resilient. Nonetheless, resilience is contextual—it is senseless without viewing it or measuring it in a context. Resilience is best tested in a crisis, as light is felt in the darkness, as warmth is experienced in the cold, and as speed is measured against stillness.

I leave the option to you to find and interpret connections and draw conclusions.

Enjoy reading your book!

Chapter One
CRISIS ANATOMIZATION

> Once upon a time, a ruminant goat set up a cud-chewing business by a mountain edge. A hoof anchored on a volatile rock, a leg suspended in the air, a knee acquired a branch, a muzzle operated the leaves, and a hoof reserved for surprises. The goat was aware of the mountain edge, the volatile rock, and the open air underneath.

Springboard

Crisis occurrences seem to have become the norm of our time. While they share a common characteristic of being moments of hardship, crises are not always identical in manifestation and progression. Hence, we cannot cure dissimilar crises with similar treatment. Crises are either nature-made or human-made. Nature-made crises are those whose causes cannot be traced back to human conduct. By exclusion, non-nature-made crises are human-made crises. Human-made crises are impacted by the prevailing conditions in nature, and nature-made crises are accentuated by human behavior. Each crisis has trigger factors and progression factors. Each crisis has a head, body, and tail. A crisis head is a pre-crisis event, a crisis body is a within-crisis event, and a crisis tail is a post-crisis event.

In this opening chapter, I use the trajectory analysis method to assess how a crisis originates and progresses. I present crisis as a symptom of an underlying disorder, as evidence of a progressive degeneration process, as a sign of issue management failure, as evidence of extreme hardship, as a symptom of an uncontrollable situation, as a manifestation of probability-impact spread, and as an opportunity to create value. Trajectory analysis is a handy tool to examine the course of a variable or an event at its terminal or stationary point. Each crisis has a specific signature. Understanding a crisis signature helps formulate intervention policies to address its underlying causes. It is like an ailment diagnosis. A wrong diagnosis may lead to inappropriate treatment, and the right diagnosis will lead to the right treatment.

From their motion angle, crises may also be classified into three categories: crises that take a process trajectory, crises that take an event trajectory, and crises that take an output trajectory. Some crises may also take on a combination of the three. A cross-cutting characteristic in all crises is that they contain an element of danger, surprise, and timeliness. [16] The danger arises from a crisis's inherent probability of personal harm or property damage. The surprise element is that crisis leaves little room for maneuvering. The timeliness is that prompt actions must be taken to contain or reverse the impact, with little or no time to think or draw plans while the crisis is unfolding.

CRISIS AS UNDERLYING DISORDER

How could a minor incident involving a lone fruit vendor in Tunisia lead to the downfall of several political regimes? How could a person in their right mind think of converting a passenger aircraft into a suicide bomb? Chaos theory offers some explanation. Chaos theory stipulates that all systems rely on underlying order, and changes to the underlying order, if not timeously addressed, generate compounded changes in the system.[17] An underlying disorder is an anomaly, a weakness, a missing piece, or a misalignment in an ecosystem. The system is visible, while the underlying order—and, consequently, any underlying disorder—is not. Think of a machine, a computer, a vehicle, a human body. Just think of anything. What you see is the system, but what keeps the system functioning are the inner parts you do not always see. A system begins cracking when parts of the underlying order malfunction. If the underlying disorder is not addressed, it triggers the malfunctioning of more underlying orders, transmitting the contagion into more underlying orders, compounding the pressure on the system, and causing the system to crash. To illustrate this with an example, imagine a minor issue such as not regularly checking your vehicle engine coolant. With time, the coolant significantly goes low and causes the engine to overheat, blowing off the engine gasket or welding the piston and cylinders. At that point, your concern is no longer topping up engine coolant but an engine replacement! In this example, topping up engine coolant is the issue causing the underlying disorder, while engine damage is the crisis resulting from not promptly addressing the disorder.

In the case of the Arab Spring, the poor Tunisian fruit vendor was a symbol of an underlying system disorder due to the malfunctioning of its inner parts. He was an aggregation of millions of inner part disorders left unaddressed for a long time. His self-inflicted harm was synonymous with tossing a matchstick into a petrol-saturated haystack. He was a manifestation of a system collapsing due to multiple internal order explosions. He was a trigger that turned a minor incident into a system-wide disruption. He symbolized a gasket that blew off due to continued ignorance of engine coolant topping up.

What is valid for political organizations is true for commercial organizations. However, in commercial organizations, a system failure triggered by internal disorders is more severe because organizations are frequently caught off-guard with no contingency plans to deal with the scale of the event—or because the incident emerges in unforeseen ways.[18] Nonetheless, resilience before a crisis will likely make an organization emerge resilient post-crisis. Likewise, post-crisis resilience will prepare an organization for the next crisis episode. For example, a smoker or an alcoholic is likely to record an above-average impact from the common cold compared to a non-smoker or a non-alcoholic. In this case, smoking and alcohol intake correspond to resilience, while the common cold refers to the crisis. Likewise, a poorly maintained neighborhood is expected to have a more devastating experience from similar flooding than a well-maintained neighborhood. Consider what a rainy day means for informal settlements compared to those living in well-planned home estates.

A crisis is not just an event but a process in a sense. Most crises begin as an anomaly that grows into a fully-fledged crisis if not addressed on time. This is known as the early developmental stage of crisis or the pre-crisis stage.[19] The Diagnostic Report issued by the 9/11 Investigative Commission revealed that warning signs about an impending act of terror on American soil were either ignored or transmitted to inter-agency services when it was already too late for action.[1] The report indicated that red flags dating back to 1993, when the first World Trade Center bombing occurred, were never taken seriously. Similarly, the Beirut explosion was not the first ammonium-nitrate disaster. In 2015, an ammonium-nitrate explosion in China claimed 150 lives, yet it seemed this was not a lesson learned for the Lebanese, as they indifferently continued to pile up chemical stocks near populated neighborhoods.[20]

Crisis happenstances as evidence of a symptomatic disorder are numerous all around us. People, corporations, sporting events, and communities all experience crises due to negligence, lack of preparedness, or myopic vision. An example of a corporate crisis as a symptomatic disorder is the collapse of Enron. While discovering fraud might have been an event, it was triggered by a corporate culture that tolerated profit over ethics.[21] Another example is the 2008 financial crisis, a symptom of regulation looseness, lack of proper oversight in the financial industry, and a culture of greed and short-term thinking.[22] The 2015 Volkswagen emissions scandal—caused by the discovery of software in their diesel cars that cheated emissions tests, leading to the release of harmful pollutants—was another symptom of poor governance disorder.[23] The International Federation of

Football Association's corruption scandal in 2015—caused by corruption and bribery within the organization—was manifested by a lack of transparency and accountability. [24] The doping scandals in professional cycling were another manifestation of a crisis as a symptomatic disorder. [25] The 2014 Flint water crisis was a symptom of government officials' lack of oversight and proper management. [26] The Grenfell Tower fire in London in 2017 was again a manifestation of tolerated negligence from using the wrong insulation material during construction. [27]

CRISIS AS PROGRESSIVE DEGENERATION

The crisis begins as a symptom of an underlying disorder, and when left unaddressed, it progresses and degenerates into a more severe problem. A crisis becomes transformative, dynamic, progressive, and terminal from that progression angle. These progression stages of a crisis are not necessarily sequential or overlapping but depend on each case.

A crisis is transformative because people's behavior after the crisis is transformed compared to their behavior before the crisis. Think of air travel nowadays. Air travel has become a painstaking process: removing shoes and belts at screening checkpoints, wearing a face mask, and not carrying more than 100 ml of liquid in cabin bags. Why? Because previous experiences transformed our behavior.

A crisis is dynamic in that it changes from one state to another over time. Crises accentuate or subside with time, sometimes without intervention and sometimes with intervention. A fire can spread or subside depending on weather conditions, rain, windspeed, vegetation, etc. An effective firefighting intervention can control the spread of fire either directly by targeting the firebase or indirectly through controlling the fire-proliferating weather conditions.

A crisis is progressive because it compounds with time. Simple solutions that can cure a crisis are no longer adequate as the crisis progresses and becomes more complex. For instance, you can take medication over the counter if you develop a mild viral infection, but if you ignore it and it develops into pneumonia, you could need to be admitted to a hospital for treatment.

The time trajectory in dynamic crises can be fast or slow, depending on the source of the crisis. Fast-unfolding crises require fast and proactive actions, while slow-unfolding crises have the benefit of lead time, enabling organizations to plan appropriately. For example, precedents in the 9/11 terror attack and the Beirut explosion indicate that authorities and organizations had time on their side, which they seemed not to have used for timely action.

A crisis is terminal at its final stationary point, indicating that the situation post-crisis is not identical to the situation before the crisis. Hence, tools, policies, procedures, logistics, and behaviors that were relevant before the crisis are sometimes irrelevant post-crisis. In practical terms, terminal crises require organizations to invest in new skills, assets, and technologies. It also implies that assets and skills explicitly acquired to deal with one crisis may not be relevant for the next crisis episode. Thus, crisis frequencies require organizations to invest in new tools and transform continually. Failure to do so makes them irrelevant at the terminal transformation stage. Think of products developed for the COVID-19 pandemic, such as facemasks, hand sanitizers, and Personal Protective Equipment. They would not be relevant for future viruses transmitted from water or food intake.

CRISIS AS ISSUE MANAGEMENT FAILURE

Issue management is detecting and handling an issue to prevent it from escalating into a crisis. An issue is any condition whose continuity will, with time, impact the performance of an ecosystem.[28] Issue management is not to be confused with crisis resolution. Issue management is a form of palliative care that does not necessarily replace full crisis resolution. It just so happens that sometimes issue management can help resolve a crisis at its earlier developmental stages, but full-fledged crises require resolution, not issue management. There has been a growing trend in organizational culture to use issue management tactics to treat mature crises. In most cases, issue management provides managers with transitional comfort while the underlying crisis keeps compounding, undisturbed. Issue management is a preventive measure to deal with the initial stages of a crisis, while crisis resolution is a curative measure that deals with a crisis at its maturity or terminal stage. Hence, crisis resolution and issue management approaches must be used within their temporal or situational relevance.

An example of issue management failure that resulted in a minor issue developing into a crisis is Johnson & Johnson's failure to address an inadequate packaging issue, which developed into a safety breach that led to product recalls, the total replacement of their packaging system, and—more critically—the loss of human lives.[29] The United

Airlines crisis, featuring a passenger dragged off a plane, was a near-perfect manifestation of how a failure to manage a minor issue can lead to widespread concern. United Airlines' reaction was perceived as slow or inadequate, and, as a result, it generated negative media coverage.[30] The 2011 Fukushima nuclear incident was caused by an earthquake and a tsunami and resulted in the failure of several nuclear reactors at the Fukushima Daiichi power plant. This could also be considered a manifestation of issue management failure. While the disaster was caused by an act of nature, the crisis management response of the plant's operator was criticized for being slow.[31] The National Football League's handling of the Ray Rice domestic violence incident in 2014 was another manifestation of a minor issue that degenerated into a crisis. The NFL was decried for failing to adequately address the situation, leading to a tarnished reputation and a decline in viewership.[32] Another example of a crisis as a manifestation of an issue management failure is the 2017 Harvey Weinstein scandal.[33] The ever-surviving movement of "MeToo" swept the world after multiple women accused Weinstein of improper behavior. Weinstein's reputation was tarnished, and the Weinstein Company failed to address the issue, leading to a share price drop.

CRISIS AS EXTREME HARDSHIP

Often, issues that are not addressed graduate into crises without warning, hence the element of surprise. Not all crises can be anticipated, and not all issues can be prevented from developing into crises.[28] A crisis at its discovery stage manifests as extreme hardship, posing an organization-wide threat.[19] Looking back at the 9/11 terrorist attack, by the time the aircraft crashed, the ground forces certainly knew nothing about the identity or intention of the hijackers. Even though aircraft hijacking is not new, using a civilian commercial airplane as a human-guided suicide bomb had no precedent in aviation history. In the same manner, while COVID-19 was not the first virus pandemic in human history, the viral signature (symptoms, progression, and prognostications) was one of the rare few occurrences in living memory. Viral DNA, a new advent in medical history, generated moments of suspense and uncertainty as the world tried to figure out how to fight the disease. The time it took to institute preventive measures, develop immune responses and vaccines, and learn to live with the virus was a time of extreme hardship.

Periods of extreme hardship tend to be Volatile, Uncertain, Ambiguous, and Complex (VUCA).[34] As the COVID-19 pandemic demonstrated, VUCA conditions render most efforts to understand the future and plan responses useless. VUCA confronts decision-makers with information insufficiency, perplexity about where to begin, and a tight timeline in which to make decisions. All the while, those involved are under pressure to have some semblance of the future and how to navigate the problems.[35] VUCA situations generate a decision paradox where tiny inputs could lead to material output, and material inputs could lead to a small or no output.[36] In the case of COVID-19, for instance, facemasks represent tiny inputs that resulted in material output, while dusk-to-down curfews could be viewed as material inputs that resulted in tiny or no output. Curfews did not effectively prevent the spread of COVID-19, while facemasks did, to a large extent. A facemask is cheap and effective in preventing viral proliferation. Dusk-to-dawn curfews are not as effective as facemasks. There are several instances where curfews resulted in crippling businesses, reducing household income,[37] freezing economic activities, increasing domestic violence against women and children,[38] creating more alcoholics, and doing little to prevent the viral spread.[39]

The frequency of crises exposes organizations to one stark reality: waiting for a return to normalcy is not a sensible proposition.[40] It is more sensible to be prepared for new and elevated waves of cataclysm rather than awaiting a return to normalcy. Any current period of extreme hardship may continue well into the future. Luckily, as crises deepen, tools to contain them are being developed in parallel. In the COVID-19 case, for instance, the world has learned how to deal with it and tackle similar occurrences in the future. But the challenge has always been that new crisis occurrences sometimes follow different trajectories and bear new signatures that call for unlearning what we know and relearning to deal with them. Please mark the words "unlearning and relearning," as they are critical in any transformation.

CRISIS AS AN UNCONTROLLABLE SITUATION

A situation out of control is typically the classic definition of a crisis.[17] Crises can escalate either from lack of preparedness or because their magnitude is more significant than the level of readiness present.[41] Lack of preparedness exhibits inadequacy, wrong preparedness, or outright unpreparedness. Whichever the case, it is a consistent observation in many crisis incidences that get out of control. Yet, timely action can redeem some aspects of damage control.[19] In the case of 9/11, the Commission Report noted that "the existing protocol was unsuited in every respect for what was about to happen."[1] Multiple problems were evident from the 9/11 disaster, most notably the passage of incomplete information and the uncoordinated response to a coordinated attack.[1] In active combat operations, the attacker is ahead of the defender most of the time. Likewise, in crimes, the criminal is (most of the time) ahead of law enforcement agencies. Hence, adaptive response methods cannot reverse the flow of a crisis, while proactive response will—to some extent. However, proactive response methods are not very popular because they entail unnecessary deployment of financial resources while an organization could be facing resource constraints.

A crisis manifestation reflects the net deficit in an organization's resilience apparatus. Most organizations today have contingency plans, but why do such plans fail to mitigate the adversities of a systemic disruption? High-impact natural disasters often overrun available defense and coping mechanisms. It was noted that many businesses and governments had insufficient buffers to cushion them against the COVID-19 economic shock.[42] The pandemic caused lots of trouble for businesses that depend on physical trading with customers. The exit of Intercontinental Hotel from some African markets after over 60 years of operation was cited as the perfect example of just how drastically COVID-19 crushed businesses across the globe, with many businesses opting to close.[43] External reinforcement intervention or out-of-the-box measures must be deployed for such organizations or systems to maintain existence.

CRISIS AS PROBABILITY-IMPACT SPREAD

Crises do not happen every day. In statistical terms, the probability of a crisis happening is low or remote. But when a crisis occurs, its negative impact on a typical organization is high. Hence, within a probability-impact spread, the impact measures crisis while probability measures its happenstance.[44] There are generally four categories of probability-impact spread: low-probability low-impact, low-probability high-impact, high-probability low-impact, and high-probability high-impact events.[45]

Probability measures the chances of an event's occurrence, while the impact measures its effect on the ecosystem if it happens. Conceptually, there is no impact without probability. Think of probability and impact as an action and consequence. Action is a probability, and the consequence is impact. A person may decide to take an action or not, but the consequence of that action will depend on whether the action is taken or not: no action, no consequence. Within the probability-impact grid, only low-probability high-impact and high-probability high-impact events are categorized as crises in this book. Low-probability low-impact events happen less frequently and have a less severe impact when they happen. Low-probability high-impact events happen less frequently but have a significant impact. High-probability low-impact events are events that happen frequently but are less severe. High-probability high-impact events are the ones that happen frequently and have severe impacts.

Most events are either low-probability low-impact, or low-probability high-impact. High-probability low-impact events are trivial matters that happen in our daily routine, such as being stopped by traffic police. Traffic police can stop you for assorted reasons, such as verifying your driving license validity, alerting you for overtaking, speeding, or turning incorrectly. But the impact of being stopped by traffic police is rarely life-threatening. High-probability high-impact events are less frequent but evident, such as the event of death. We all know that we shall all die one day (high probability), and when it occurs, we cease to exist (high impact).

Low-probability high-impact events represent a tricky situation for organizational leaders due to an inherent belief that low probability makes crises happenstances somehow remote. For example, when traveling by air, we frequently listen to recorded safety protocols aboard aircraft, repeating "in the unlikely event of cabin pressure failure," "in the unlikely event of landing in water," and so on. The expression "in the unlikely event" denotes low probability, but its corresponding impact could be disastrous. Aircraft are known to be the safest means of travel nowadays. However, stressing the unlikelihood of a disaster gives passengers a false sense of safety. Some planes land in the water, as they have landed before. Some planes crash, as indeed planes have crashed, and some cabin pressure fails, as indeed they have failed before.

Stressing the low-probability aspect of a crisis provides a false sense of safety, induces complacency, diverts resources away from preparedness, and heightens crisis impact. What is the rationale behind corporate fire drills? Fire preparedness, yes. Fire drills, no. Why? Typifying fire alarms at intervals domesticates responsiveness, repels fear, tames surprise, and emasculates agility. Readers are familiar with evacuees reacting negatively to frequent fire drills by not taking matters seriously. By the way, "fire drill" is a metaphor for firefighting behavior as a subsistence tactic, signifying a managerial attitude that only cares about what must be done today; tomorrow takes care of itself!

Low-probability high-impact events happen occasionally, and most crises affecting organizations are isolated events. For some organizations, the COVID-19 pandemic represented the first major high-impact crisis ever experienced in their lifetime.[46] While this is the case, continuous communication of crises as low-probability events potentially confers a false sense of safety. Similarly, preaching crises as high-impact events confers a false sense of helplessness. If managers believe crises are highly impactful, irrespective of remedial actions, why should they prepare? A careful balancing act is therefore called for.

CRISIS AS A VALUE-CREATION OPPORTUNITY

While a crisis conventionally connotes adversity, considering a crisis as synonymous with a threat is a minimalistic approach that limits organizational resilience potential. Beyond being prepared to cope with the adverse effects of a crisis, some organizations capitalize on the crisis to realize growth. Most crises have an element of duality: opportunities and threats. Positive leaders see a glass half-filled, while negative leaders see it half-empty. Each party gets what they see.[36]

Crisis-benefiting organizations fall into two categories: profit-making organizations and growth-realizing organizations. Examples of profit-making organizations were numerous in the wake of the COVID-19 pandemic. During the COVID-19 pandemic, digital conferencing companies significantly gained from the lockdown as business was conducted virtually.[47] As the pandemic subsided and lockdowns gradually eased, most organizations quickly returned to physical business interaction. Consequently, digital conferencing services could not keep the same profit levels. This was a CIPMO. On the other hand, vaccine manufacturers had CIGRO. They invested in equipment elastic to industrial output demand that can be customized to produce sustainable demand-driven products. Vaccine manufacturers also realized critical growth in human capital assets, research and development, and reputational capital.[48]

CIPMO and CIGRO are manifestations of leaders' abilities to orchestrate organizational resources.[49] Resources pass through three stages: raw resources, functional resources, and capabilities. Raw resources are in the possession of all types of organizations. Functional resources are promoted resources that organizational leaders manage to convert into value-generating resources through deliberate leadership actions. Capabilities are the highest level of resources that leaders manage to promote from functional resources through deliberate strategies.[50]

Sequentially, leaders orchestrate raw resources into functional resources and promote functional resources into capabilities. By the same corollary, capabilities may be demoted into functional resources and functional resources demoted into raw resources through leadership inaction or bad actions. One could argue that resource promotion and resource demotion is one phenomenon that explains inter-organizational resilience differential. Therefore, CIPMO and CIGRO are manifestations of resilience capabilities to induce compounded value to organizational resources. Those organizations with compounded capabilities are on autopilot mode, seamlessly responding to crises and disruptive shocks by reconfiguring their capabilities to maintain performance and growth irrespective of the underlying conditions.[51] In my prior work, the concept of CIPMO and CIGRO was extended to classify organizations into three categories based on leadership's ability to orchestrate raw resources into functional resources and promote functional resources into capabilities.[49] I use the livestock analogy to classify organizations into cow, camel, and goat organizations.

When drought hits, cows typically die first, followed by camels, while goats often survive and prosper. Cow organizations sit on raw resources they cannot exploit to the limit. They have the size, the weight, and the power but are useless in drought. Camel organizations convert raw resources into functional resources, and that is it. They have height and endurance but also have a restricted dietary regime, a clear disadvantage when pastures are limited due to drought. Goat organizations promote functional resources into capabilities by continually finding new uses for the functional resources at their disposal. They do not necessarily have the size advantage but are very agile.

Goat organizations see a crisis as a value-creation opportunity, no matter how hidden. They are unafraid to take risks and try new things. Their agility is unmatched. They possess a sixth sense of sniffing out opportunities. They survive and thrive beyond disruption, primarily due to their agility, openness to dietary habits, and risk-taking behaviors. A goat could be spotted creeping by the mountain edge with one leg anchored onto a volatile rock, one leg suspended in the air, two legs pulling a tree branch, and a mouth doing the job on the leaves. The goat is aware of the mountain edge, the volatile rock, and the open air underneath. What does that mean for organizations? While the harsh winds of change are taking down the cows, goats are busy chowing down on every opportunity they can find. Camels see themselves through the crisis but are never as nimble as goats. Camels are content in just getting by, but goats always look for ways to improve and grow.

Are you a corporate leader? You can transform your cow into a camel and transform your camel into a goat. But you can also regress a goat organization to a camel and a camel organization to a cow. Let us make a choice and learn resilience resource orchestration from the goat!

Self-Cascading Reflections

Let us reflect for a moment on the concept of crisis as an underlying disorder and relate it to our own organizational or personal crisis experience. In retrospect, let us identify the underlying disorder or disorders that led to the crisis we have experienced in our personal or professional lives. Let us now reflect on the following questions:

- What factors contributed to the underlying disorder?

- Which disorders were human-made, and which ones were made by nature/machine/system?
- What lessons do we learn from the progressions of the underlying disorders?
- In hindsight, what would have been done differently to prevent the crisis?
- What could have been done differently to minimize its impact?
- What simple solutions could have prevented the crisis but turned inadequate as the crises became more complex?
- What profit-making opportunities could we have identified?
- Which profit-making opportunities did we miss?
- What growth-realizing opportunities could we have identified?
- Which growth-realizing opportunities were missed?
- How did our organization exploit these opportunities, if at all?
- Are we or our organization a goat, a camel, or a cow?
- What could we have done to transform our organization?
- In hindsight, what could have been done differently to exploit the opportunities?

Bend Your Mind!

The MeToo movement, born out of Harvey Weinstein's improper behavior and similar incidents, was a crisis manifestation of an issue management failure. But why was it such a short-lived one?

The MeToo movement did not reach far as a moment of inflection for women's rights. The MeToo movement should have gone down history in a comparable way to Martin Luther King Jr.'s "I Have a Dream," to Nelson Mandela's "I Am Prepared to Die," and to Ronald Reagan's "Tear Down This Wall." It should have marked the road sign for the lasting emancipation of women worldwide from violence, trafficking, mutilation, and unequal pay. The MeToo movement did not push for worldwide legislation, although women held influential positions. The MeToo may have faded quickly because it was built around a case, not a cause. A movement needs not to be built around an issue. It is like labor unions asking for a pay rise.

Did the MeToo movement lack visionary leadership? Maybe. Maybe not. Should it have been a global movement? Probably. Should it have used sexual exploitation to symbolize overall injustice against women? I wished so. One would have imagined the women's movement as a cause-driven organization like the Rotary and Freemasons. Their unique organizational culture, established over decades, preserved and transferred across generations, and their organizational prowess, secretive or non, is an anchor testimony of how movements can be built around a cause. A Women's Movement for Emancipation and Normalization (WOMEN) should have somehow come out against Male Egoistic Narcissism (MEN). It remains women's choice. You get the point.

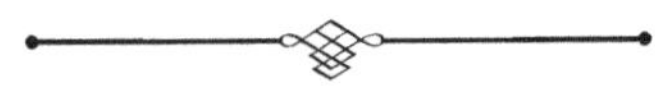

Chapter Two

RESILIENCE DISSECTION

> Drawing a linear plan in a changing environment is like painting on a dry valley bed stone, knowing too well that the stone will submerge in an imminent inundation. As the flood recedes, the algae trace on the redeemed stone recounts a story of an erstwhile fallaciously cheered plan.

Springboard

A story is told of a bridge to nowhere.

The New Choluteca Bridge became the talk of online media. It was a robust bridge that endured a devastating hurricane that ravaged Honduras the same year the bridge was opened. The story dates to 1998 when Hurricane Mitch wreaked havoc over the Caribbean—described as Central America's worst hurricane in over 200 years. In total, 150 bridges collapsed. Knowing the bridge was likely to face extreme weather conditions, the Honduran government commissioned some of the best architectural brains to build a bridge that could withstand any hurricane.[52] While the New Choluteca Bridge remained unscathed, there was a new problem. The access roads to the bridge disappeared, and the Choluteca River, which necessitated the building of the bridge in the first place, changed course after the disaster. It was no longer flowing under the bridge. The bridge, standing over dry land with no connecting roads on either side, was rendered useless the same year it was ready for use.

The Honduran government may have done everything right to the extent humanly possible. The strategy was planned and executed all the way to the bridge. But the bridge needed another bridge—or, in the terms of Martin Reeves, the strategy required a strategy.[53]

But quite effectively, the strategy may have lost its practical relevance due to being hailed in a herd-style manner. The strategy morphed from a means to an end into an end in its own right. Strategy has transformed from stepwise pragmatic action plans into some form of entitlement to elitism in the corporate world. The word "strategy" may have been used in recent memory, deliberately or inadvertently, in a way that made it feel non-negotiable and a must-have at any cost. The strategy became a brand that ranks organizations within the elites of their club. The downside of a must-have strategy is that the strategy becomes a box-ticking syndrome. A strategy that does not incorporate resilience is void in sense and form. A strategy that is not based on contingencies and backup options is a corporate public relation exercise. A strategy that seeks comfort and avoids asking tough questions is heading to the trash bin.

In this section, I discuss a resilience-flavored strategy and attempt to present it as an alternative approach to conventional corporate strategizing. In so doing, I revisit strategy construction elements and infuse them with recipes of resilience. Hence, this chapter explores resilience as a contingency planning tool, as a resilience strategy anchor, and as a sustainability management tool.

RESILIENCE AS CONTINGENCY PLANNING

As early as 1988, Arthur D. Little questioned the rationale and the sense of doing a strategy. He questioned the usefulness of engaging in strategic reviews, analyzing market positions, and setting goals and tactics where the world changes by the time organizations finish their goalsetting activities.[54] In 1990, Henry Mintzberg cast aspersions into the magic bullet of strategic management in his book, *The Rise and Fall of Strategic Planning*.[55] Since the turn of the 21st century, the question of whether strategic management is relevant to current organizational challenges has found its way into corporate conversations time and again, with no compelling answer.

Emeritus Professor Franklin of Nottingham Trent University posed the same question in 2001.[56] While the professor responded with an emphatic "yes," the question is still being asked two decades later. Some may even wonder whether the question is worth their time since the very concept and process of strategic planning became the solution for managers increasingly faced with environmental chaos. Thus, they needed some sense of order in how their organization's position in such environments could be evaluated with coherence.[57]

The value of strategic planning has been affirmed in various management literature as the surest way to sustain competitiveness in today's volatile and uncertain world.[58] Well, is that true? The antithesis to this well-established standpoint is just as compelling for the following reasons.

Firstly, discontinuous alteration undermines the holding power of existing strategies. Sometimes, "organizational environments undergo cataclysmic upheavals—changes so sudden and extensive that they alter the trajectories of entire industries, overwhelm the adaptive capacities of resilient organizations, and surpass the comprehension of seasoned managers."[59] If your business survives on consumer taste and is susceptible to tech disruption, you are familiar with the progression and impact of such upheavals. When your next-door neighbor migrates, you could be next. Commodore International Corporation, a successful desktop company in the 1970s and 80s, went under in 1994 because consumer taste shifted under their watch while company leaders failed to see it coming.[60]

Secondly, when such discontinuity occurs with increased frequency, strategic plans often face obsolescence before being fully implemented. There is a generally wrong perception that good strategies are complex ideas expressed in extravagant language, looking into the future (reflecting the sound vision of our founding fathers!). Really? Good strategies are *simple* strategies. Military strategists know that good conduct in war is not to risk it all but, if necessary, to be able to retreat, reposition, and return. Likewise, corporate leaders may need to take a 360-degree view when laying out strategies and make assumptions as close to real-life situations as possible.

Thirdly, environmental uncertainty and complexity transcend human cognitive power that informs predictions and scenario analysis typical of classical strategic planning and review processes. Thus, the critical option is to be prepared for all eventualities. This is a more lustrous option than having a plan that does not stand the test of the next shock.

Lastly, the blurring of industry boundaries makes it difficult to estimate and effectively counter new sources of competitive disruption and asymmetric threats using conventional strategic management tools.[61] Take a moment to think of AI-induced technological disruption. Is it still a sound judgment to adopt, for instance, a sales growth strategy whereby the company's sales grow by, say, 5 percent for the next five years? The driving force of product discovery is consumer taste, right? But what drives consumer taste? Product discovery, right? So, we are in this circular spiral: consumer taste prompts new products, and new products change consumer taste. Sometimes consumer taste changes before the new product lands on the market; thus, it is obsolete before it hits shelves. Another new product may have used an updated consumer prediction model that rubbished the first product. Drawing a constant-assumption strategy in a changing and challenging environment is like painting on a dry valley stone, knowing too well that the rock will be submerged in an imminent inundation. In such cases, and many other similar cases, strategic planning becomes a form of box-ticking to provide corporate managers with an ephemeral sense of safety and accomplishment.

The unease surrounding strategic planning becomes apparent with the widely held practice of long-range planning as a strategic management practice.[62] Long-range planning has often been used as a substitute for strategic planning.

[63] Yet, as the COVID-19 pandemic and other significant events of the 21st century have demonstrated, such plans barely sustain relevance past their third year of implementation. For many organizations, conducting strategic reviews has become necessary, sometimes as frequently as annually. [64] When such strategic plans are retired, the difference between what is realized and what was planned is worlds apart. This traditional worldview of strategic management often neither prevents a crisis nor protects corporates from the most damaging developments.[65]

RESILIENCE AS MANAGEMENT STRATEGY

There are good traditions enshrined in strategic management literature. Strategic management tools such as Political-Economic-Social-Technological-Environmental-Legal analysis (PESTEL) and Strengths-Weaknesses-Opportunities-Threats (SWOT) are geared toward detecting not only the looming dangers and advantages presented by the operating environment but also the areas of strengths and internal organizational weaknesses. Situational analysis is an essential first step to preparedness—a crucial element of dynamic resilience, i.e., crisis resilience.

A question that would be asked is: why SWOT? Think of the combination of SWOT against the combination of strengths-opportunities-weakness-threats (SOWT). The former sounds more logical, considering the causational direction of events that characterize organizations operating in dynamic environments. However, I argue here that strengths attract opportunities, and opportunities support corporate strength. Weakness exposes the organization to threats, which undermine the organization, leading to more weakness. Not exploiting opportunities is a weakness that prevents corporations from exploiting new opportunities. Thus, SOWT is a more suitable reordering of the framework, as SOWT potentially better activates an organization's resilience faculties.

Beyond sequential relevance, the reordering from SWOT to SOWT has practical implications for policy and operation prioritization in disruptive times. When organizations face challenging situations, limited resources must be devoted to consolidating strength. As the famous American proverb attributed to John F. Kennedy's father suggests, when the going gets tough, it is the tough who get going. For instance, during tough times, organizations with solid financial and reputational assets are better positioned to exploit opportunities that arise from crises. In contrast, a weak organization is not set up to leverage opportunities brought by the winds of change. By reordering the framework, the focus is shifted to the combination of internal and external environmental factors that an organization should prioritize.

A crisis is defined as an event, which means we can model resilience as a situational analysis around the event: pre-event, within-event, and post-event. Thus, presenting crisis as a stationary point and resilience as a cluster of dynamic actions around the crisis allows for convergence between strategic leadership and resilience leadership. This book does not advocate throwing the baby out with the bathwater. Instead, it converges resilience and strategic leadership to yield an optimal equilibrium between management, strategy, emergence, and resilience. This convergence is termed (MASTER) in this book, where "MA" stands for management, "ST" stands for strategy, "E" stands for emergence, and "R" stands for resilience.

The concept of MASTER combines emergent strategy with deliberate strategy or pragmatic strategy. It fuses proactive, adaptive, and anticipatory resilience into a unified powerhouse. It comingles strategy with operations. It entails keeping an eye on the horizon while attending to daily preoccupations. It means the ability to reshuffle resources smartly toward the most critical objectives of an organization. In short, it is a resilience strategy. It resembles an automobile engine's Variable Valve Timing-Intelligent (VVT-I). Intelligent valves adjust air and fuel intake timing by applying the oil pressure to change the camshaft position, alternating the tension between the intake valve and the shaft, and enabling the vehicle to distribute power efficiently relative to the drive terrain. The concept of MASTER acts for organizations in the same way as VVT-I for smart-engined vehicles, allowing organizational leadership to distribute and redistribute resources, priorities, policies, and capabilities where value is continuously maximized to enable the organization to maintain sustained resilience.

What is the consequence of merging operations with planning? I am referring to both functional and structural merging. It means a potential new configuration of the organization's structure such that it can continuously and seamlessly blend operations with planning, profit with growth, present with future, strategy with resilience, and leadership with management. It means the potential emergence of new organizations that can steer core values to new horizons and withstand cataclysms.

Does it sound idealistic? Gareth Morgan presented metaphors for different organization types. Morgan argued that some organizations look like machines, others like organisms, brains, or cultural or political systems. Others are psychic prisons, and some are instruments of domination. [66] This book similarly used a livestock analogy to depict goat, cow, and camel organizations. One would argue that Morgan's old clips and stereotypes may be too old and narrow to contain modern organizational metaphors. Looking around today, you could spot vampiric organizations (that survive by sucking the blood of taxpayers), dinosaurous organizations (that outlive their time), hypersonic organizations (that grow out of proportion in a blink of an eye), cybernetic organizations (that only exist in the virtual world), tortoisic organizations (that never transform), and futuristic organizations (that have excellent market forecasts).

For now, let us gradually build the elements of a resilient organization, starting with introducing the concept of organizational capability, which is closely related to the idea of MASTER.

A re-imagination of strategic management began just before the turn of the New Millennium when Professor David Teece and his research team introduced the concept of dynamic capabilities view (DCV). Hailed as a new paradigm in strategic management, the DCV proposition was advanced on the notion that winning organizations "demonstrate timely responsiveness, rapid product innovation, and management capability."[67] Accordingly, dynamic capabilities represent an organization's capacity to "combine, develop and reconfigure external and internal resources to respond speedily to a changing environment."[67] A classic example of dynamic capabilities often quoted in strategy textbooks is the development of the iPod by Apple. Apple seized an opportunity from consumer dissatisfaction with traditionally bulky MP3 players and introduced an aesthetically appealing alternative, effectively transforming the main Apple industry line into a consumer electronics brand.

DCV comprises three phases: anticipation, coping, and adaptation capabilities.[68] Recall that resilience is defined and measured in this book as a dynamic trajectory around crisis: pre-crisis resilience (anticipatory resilience), within-crisis resilience (proactive resilience), and post-crisis resilience (adaptive resilience). In a sense, organizational capability mirrors crisis-resilience capability. Anticipation capabilities entail risk forecasting to inform decisions that must be made now to circumvent future disruptions. They entail environmental scanning, identifying critical threats, and developing response mechanisms to counter expected and unexpected occurrences of disruption. Coping capabilities involve swinging plans into actions and developing and implementing ad-hoc solutions. They depend on possession or access to resources that promote firm survival because they can be easily transformed and reconfigured. Adaptive capabilities comprise advancement strategies, such as the organizational transformation and learning required to respond more effectively to future crises.[69]

DCV was premised mainly on the inherent assumption that disruption only emanates from industry forces and ignores the forces triggered by nature. For this reason, increasingly disruptive events have interrogated the relevance of DCV. Hence, transitioning from deliberate strategic management with DCV as its primary legacy tool toward resilience leadership constitutes a paradigm shift in management practice.[51] The increased frequency and intensity of natural disasters informed the Honduran government to build the New Choluteca Bridge. Yet, the aftermath of the hurricane demonstrated that surprises are multifaceted, sudden, and often incomprehensible.[70] While they knew that a disaster would undoubtedly happen at some point, the Honduran government and the engineers who built the bridge did not know when and how it would unfold. Such happenstances challenge corporate management to develop and test alternative postulations that promise a more resilient explanation for organizational sustainability that legacy theoretical models like DCV have not adequately addressed.

The starting point in the paradigm shift from strategic management toward resilience leadership is a redefinition of "resilience." Perhaps the building of the New Choluteca Bridge was informed by a narrow structural engineering definition of resilience as "the ability to withstand shocks."[71] This connotes a system's robustness. As it turned out, it was not enough that the bridge was robust. Considering the lessons therein, it helps to redefine resilience as "continued usefulness in the face of adversity." This definition draws inspiration from psychology, which defines resilience as "dynamic and positive adaptation."[72]

An expanded definition of resilience applicable to a broad range of disciplines is "the capacity of a dynamic system to adapt successfully to disturbances that threaten system function, viability, or development."[73] This means that for a system to be qualified as resilient, it needs to be dynamic, functioning, and viable. The three aspects are entangled and mutually reinforcing, as a dynamic system enables an organization to adjust to temporal challenges while being functional allows an organization to fulfill its purpose of existence. Finally, being viable empowers an organization to adapt to uncertainties. The hurricane revealed that the New Choluteca Bridge lacked all these critical aspects of resilience. It was no longer functioning and viable without additional investment and was also not dynamic. As a corollary to the New Choluteca Bridge case, organizations that do not possess the three properties are not resilient. Resilient organizations responsively and timely adapt their business models and strategies to emergent environmental realities to sustain relevance.[74]

This book presents resilience leadership as an organization-wide governing strategy geared toward value creation. Resilience management combines business continuity, adaptability, and opportunity management.[75] Business continuity management is a well-established practice in modern corporate life. It provides a framework for resilience building toward staging an effective response to safeguard value preservation and creation activities.[76]

Adaptability management is a new element of resilience management introduced in this book, and it is defined as the creation and optimization of the fluidity needed to attain fitness for emergent purposes. Opportunity management refers to applying the concept of risk management to the identification, analysis, treatment, and evaluation of possible opportunities based on the risk-opportunity duality. [77] Opportunities are positive consequences of disruption. Research evidence suggests that some businesses realize extraordinary returns and flourish during disruption. For example, while some retail traders in China incurred losses during the COVID-19 lockdown, others thrived.[78] Similar findings have been reported in Kenya, where some SMEs generated windfall revenues from COVID-19. Resilience management aims to create organizational shock absorbers (enhancing resistance) and preserve elements that foster rapid organizational self-renewal, self-recreation, and self-reinvention following a disruption. If effectively implemented, the four core pillars of resilience management represent a management co-pilot that puts organizations on autopilot mode for effective and sustainable resilience.

This book introduces the idea of organizational resilience as a deliberate emergent strategy (a deliberate emergent strategy refers to strategic preparedness for, learning from, and responsiveness to change). In my earlier work, organizational resilience was defined comprehensively as the process and outcome of strategic preparedness for disruption, adaptive response to disruption, capitalizing on disruption, organizational survival, positive transformation, and prosperity.[79]

Strategic preparedness is about recognizing turbulence as the new normal and, therefore, the importance of approaching organizational resilience as a strategic issue. Preparedness is an all-encompassing concept for anticipating the expected and the unexpected, resilience planning, monitoring, and stress-testing.

Adaptive response is about orchestrating dynamic resources with the agility and swiftness needed to minimize the adverse effects of disruption and maximize opportunities that present themselves. Adaptive response appreciates the reality that disruption is not only sometimes unavoidable but can also present advantages that necessitates adjustments to the status quo.

Capitalizing on disruption is about sensing and seizing every opportunity that comes with adversity. Organizational survival is a generic term for the ability to withstand and recover from disruption. Positive transformation is the progressive process and outcome of dynamic resource orchestration for enhanced market readiness in an uncertain world. Prosperity is simply about thriving and growth despite market realities.

RESILIENCE AS SUSTAINABILITY MANAGEMENT

The ultimate source of corporate resilience and sustainable competitive advantage does not accrue from a firm's strategic resources but from how management and leadership actively and dynamically blend and orchestrate the existing stock of dynamic resources, thereby creating additional marginal capabilities from the resource blend.[69] This applies to all levels of organizations: corporations, states, cooperatives, charities, etc. Countless examples of organizations around us flourished with limited resources because leadership applied creative dynamic capabilities to transform the limited resources into strategic growth drivers. Organizations that orchestrate dynamic resources set themselves up with the agility to survive and thrive during disruptions.

The sustainability management strategy in a typical organization aims to protect its valuable ecosystems.[80] Let us take the global banking marketplace as an example to demonstrate the inextricable linkage between organizations and their ecosystem and to illustrate that organizational resilience is a sustainability management strategy. The 2008 global financial crisis symbolized a defining moment in the banking space. On the negative side, the ensuing recession reversed significant gains that had been made toward achieving Sustainable Development Goal 1—an end to poverty in all its forms. The financial crisis triggered a severe rise in the global poverty headcount and stifled progress toward realizing some of the Sustainable Development Goals (SDG).[81] On the positive side, the crisis unsettled the business environment and activated an unparalleled strengthening of stress-testing systems to augment banking sector resilience worldwide.[82] After the recession, significant efforts were made to buffer capital adequacy and supervisory procedures to boost the banking system's resilience. From a global perspective, the mutation of risk profiling within the banking ecosystem prompted drastic scrutiny measures to safeguard stakeholder value, such as capital adequacy standards, anti-money laundering procedures, and know your customer requirements.

Due to the contingent nature of banks' balance sheets, it became paramount to enhance shareholders' skin in the game by deepening capital metrics, given their loss-absorbing property. For instance, in the wake of the 2008 financial crisis, America's banking authorities coordinated the resilience of its banking assets by triggering increased capitalization and reduced dependence on short-term funding.[83] Advancement has also been remarkable from the financial reforms angle in Africa, with the continent's banking system recording significantly fewer occurrences of systemic shocks than the global average. Using Kenya as an example, the crisis prompted regulatory authorities to increase banks' core capital by 300 percent with a four-year deadline, which materially strengthened the latent resilience of Kenya's financial industry.[84] When the COVID-19 health crisis struck more than a decade later, banks worldwide became the first resort for global economic resilience, thanks to multiple layers of efforts invested in strengthening the resilience of the worldwide banking ecosystem over the years.[85] Analysts argued that capital adequacy and increased prudential minimums significantly enhanced the banking system's resilience to systemic disruption. Specifically, prudential requirements saw banks raise their capital ratios, which became an effective resilience response to the COVID-19-related economic shocks.[86]

Self-Cascading Reflections

The New Choluteca Bridge story shows how organizational environments undergo cataclysmic upheavals and changes so sudden and extensive that they alter the trajectories of entire industries, overwhelm the adaptive capacities of resilient organizations, and surpass the comprehension of seasoned managers. As we reflect on the New Choluteca Bridge, let us take a moment to recall instances where we felt that, as leaders, we had done everything right, but the results simply did not add up for us. Let us now reflect on the following questions:

- What are the dark spots that we may have overlooked?
- What lessons did we learn to improve our resilience and preparedness?

- How can we adopt deliberate policies to improve our adaptive resilience?
- How can we take a holistic approach to resilience management and ensure that all dimensions of resilience are covered?
- How can we learn from our successes and failures to build resilience and continuously improve our resilience management processes over time?
- What alternative resilience options should our organization adopt to strengthen its strategic preparedness for novel crises?

Bend Your Mind!

The universe is exceptionally resilient. Physics informs us that the Earth rotates around itself at 1,056 mph (1700 km/h) and orbits the sun at 66,000 mph (107,000 km/h). The sun and the solar system move in the Milky Way—our home galaxy—at 497 mph (800 km/h). The Milky Way moves in the universe at 1.2 million mph (2 million km/h). The universe expands at 150,993 mph (243,000 km/h). Now, while considering the motion of the Earth, the solar system, the Milky Way, and the universe, think of Earth as a vehicle and you and I as passengers. How fast are we moving, even while watching a cricket match from the comfort of our sitting room? It is like traveling in a plane—you do not feel the plane moving, even though you are cruising at 559 mph (900 km/h). The size of the observable universe is estimated at 95 billion light years. In other words, it takes us 95 billion years to cross the universe from edge to edge if we travel at the speed of light. As you think of this massive structure, the infinite sub-structures it contains, the staggering speed of motions of each sub-structures, the orderliness of their motions, and the sustenance of their existence beyond the boundaries of space and time, you can only submit to the power of the Power holding them together.

Chapter Three
CRISIS-CYCLE RESILIENCE TRAITS

> As one gains altitude over the clouds of self, one perceives a fairer version of self.

Springboard

At the dawn of a peaceful Friday, February 15, 2013, a meteor 62 feet (19 meters), shooting at a staggering speed of 41,631 mph (67,000 km/h), entered the Earth's atmosphere over the Ural region in Russia.[87] At entry, it produced kinetic energy equivalent to 500 kilotons of TNT, equaling 33 times the energy released from the Hiroshima bomb detonation. Luckily, the meteor incinerated at 19 mi (30 km) above sea level.[88] Even so, the ensuing sonic boom damaged 7,000 buildings, injured 1,500 people, interrupted gas supply in some districts, and destroyed a nearby factory.[89] Had the meteor exploded in Chelyabinsk, the impact would have been apocalyptic because the city is densely populated.[90] The National Aeronautics and Space Administration (NASA) estimates that a meteor measuring 459 feet (140 meters) in length could wipe out an entire city. A meteor measuring 60 miles (96 km) could wipe out life on Earth. The asteroid that decimated the dinosaur population 66 million years ago was estimated to be six miles (ten kilometers) in size.[91]

While a meteor impacting Earth is a low-probability event by the Earth's standards, businesses experience high-probability impact events with increasing and recurring episodes of disruptive shocks. Disruption is bound to happen repeatedly, with or without notice. The frequency of disruptive episodes implies that organizations are continually in the middle of a disruption, out of a disruption, or preparing for a disruption. Because disruptions are cyclical, organizations must continuously be alert and remain resilient before, during, and after crises. At each crisis phase, organizations need to adopt specific traits, keeping in mind that traits relevant at one stage are not necessarily relevant at another. In this chapter, I explore how resilience manifests in various stages of a crisis and analyze resilience traits at each crisis stage.

CRISIS-RESILIENCE CONTINUITY

There are two fundamental characteristics of the crisis-resilience combination. The first characteristic is that a crisis passes through three phases: pre-crisis, within-crisis, and post-crisis. The second characteristic is that resilience is measured against a crisis. No crisis, no test of resilience. Hence, resilience passes through three phases: pre-crisis resilience, within-crisis resilience, and post-crisis resilience.

Which phase comes first is a chicken-and-egg situation. Logical intuition implies that crises begin with pre-crisis (crisis head), progress to within-crisis (crisis body), and end at the post-crisis stage (crisis tail). Fortunately, or unfortunately, this logic does not apply to crises. Crises occur without forewarning. Therefore, the starting point of a crisis is its manifestation (within-crisis or crisis body), not its precursor (pre-crisis or crisis head) or its terminal (post-crisis or crisis tail). Crises are cyclical.

Let us take an example to illustrate this. Assume three crises: crises A, B, and C. If the three crises occur in succession, then cyclically, crisis A is pre-crisis with respect to crises B and C. Crisis B is post-crisis with respect to crisis A and pre-crisis with respect to crisis C. Crisis C is post-crisis with respect to crises A and B, but at the same time, it is within-crisis with respect to crises A and B, *and* pre-crisis with respect to crisis A.

In aggregate, each crisis is pre-crisis, within-crisis, and post-crisis. In other words, crises are cyclical. Thus, resilience is cyclical as well. In the earlier example, if crisis A is before B, and B is before C, then A is before C. If C is after A, and A is after B, then C is after B. If B is between A and C, and C is between A and B, then A, B, and C move within a cycle, indicating that organizations are in a crisis-cycle continually. Consider that crises are evenly spaced at infinity, i.e., normally distributed.[92] If we further assume that an organization exists for (n) years and it experiences (c) number of crises, and we represent crises interval by (k), then the time an organization is in crisis (y) may be expressed in this simple equation:

$$y = c * k / n.^{(49)}$$

The expression c*k measures crisis intensity, i.e., the number of crises multiplied by each crisis interval. In this simple equation, y increases with c and k and decreases with n. In other words, time in crisis is a positive function of crisis severity and a negative function of operational longevity. It means, theoretically, that the longer an organization has been operational, the less severe the impact of successive crises on that organization. Operational longevity could indicate a learning curve, enabling organizations to better deal with repeated crisis episodes. Since organizations are continually in a crisis cycle, they must be continually resilient. This chapter will discuss desirable resilience traits organizations require at the crisis's three stages: pre-crisis, within-crisis, and post-crisis.

WITHIN-CRISIS RESILIENCE TRAITS

Resilience at the within-crisis stage is the most critical of the three stages. Crises function as a litmus test for an organization's resilience and often come without forewarning. So, most organizations only know they are in crisis when it happens. Positive reframing, improvisation, flexibility, and collaboration are organizational traits that serve as resilience anchors during a crisis.

Positive Reframing

Positive reframing is an intentional leadership act of looking into adverse situations from a positive lens. Adverse situations require an extra dose of positivity to overcome.

Most people tend to get frustrated when faced with adverse situations. Frustration freezes our creativity and prevents us from finding the best options to overcome adversity. Frustration delivers a twin blow to our spirit: a blow from adversity and a self-inflicted blow from our own frustration. In adverse situations, if you can overcome your self-inflicted frustration, you are left with only one problem: the adverse situation. Being positive comes powerfully to our rescue as it gives us extra internal strength to think, clears our spirits to make sound judgments, and encourages us to keep exploring all options until we arrive at a better resolution. Positive reframing is not for the faint-hearted, as it goes against our human nature: we are expected to be emotional, hurt, angry, and crying, is normal. But if we keep our composure and develop cool heads around adversity, we will make an enormous difference in our lives and those around us.

To develop positive-reframing skills, we need to develop self-fairness. Self-fairness is the ability to suppress our self-love tendency. It is the ability to exit our soul and address ourselves in a second-person pronoun. Once we exit our self-confinements, we can reign over ourselves. If we get frustrated and begin shouting, becoming agitated, or crying, we need an external source to call us to reason. We can create that external source from our own selves through self-fairness.

Positive reframing is a well-established psychological concept with broad applications in business. It is viewing a negative situation in a positive spirit. It is tantamount to seeing a glass half-full, not half-empty. Positive reframing means having hope in the darkest moments. It is recognized as one of the most effective coping mechanisms for surviving personal adversity.[93]

In organizational resilience, positive reframing takes on a new level of meaning, not just managing adversity but recognizing an opportunity in adversity. It is the ability to view a silver lining in every dark cloud and extract it to the organization's advantage. In every adversity lies an opportunity—but we often cannot see the opportunity because adversity blurs our vision. Albert Einstein said that amid every crisis lies excellent opportunity.[94] Opportunity exploitation in times of crisis can be equated to fully harnessing all the possibilities occasioned by disruptive events to transition an organization and its people into a thriving enterprise.[95] A failure to seek opportunity in crisis may pose an existential threat to organizations.

Improvisation

Improvisation refers to taking actions without rehearsal. It is the ultimate bravery of leadership action. In abrupt and sudden disruptions where time to think becomes a liability, someone must shout: "Let's move." Improvisation is a resilience trait that entails spontaneously responding to incidences by reorganizing the disposable resources to sustain vital functions until the danger is minimized or terminated. It requires an out-of-the-box mindset, stubbornness, and bravery to go against the crowd and pull hearts and minds to your side.

Captain Chesley Sullenberger, the commander of Flight 1549—fondly known as Captain Sully—was forced to land on the River Hudson after a collision with a flock of geese. He improvised a safety solution by landing the plane on the water.[96] Captain Sully had no time to look for an airfield;

he saw a water runway instead and landed thereon. Surgeons often face improvisational situations at the theater when a decision must be made that involves either losing the patients or saving their lives. The doctor has no time to hold a meeting. Any moment wasted is irreversible. Military commanders also face similar situations on the battlefield. Commanders have to decide whether to defend or retreat. If they decide to defend, they must do so with the resources at their disposal. They cannot wait for reinforcement because they cannot predict the adversary's move. That decision from the commander could wipe out the entire contingent. But the commander takes full responsibility, including risks of court-martial. At times, an organizational leader must put on the skin of an army commander, a surgeon, or a pilot. Improvisation needs no prior training; it needs a single, most critical leadership attribute: measured bravery.[97]

Improvisation is critical for corporations at the crisis manifestation stage, as it allows them to adapt to changing circumstances and capitalize on new opportunities quickly. The COVID-19 pandemic is a prime example of the importance of improvisation, as many companies have had to pivot their business models to survive the pandemic.

Flexibility

Flexibility is the ability to self-reinvent in response to market needs. Flexible organizations efficiently reconfigure resources in response to changes in the operating environment. Crises generate market disruptions that lead to high variability in demand and supply, impacting the nature and uses of products, process dynamics, and the shelf-life of inputs. Flexibility is an organization-wide attribute that transcends all operational and administrative spheres: operations, supply chain, business model, machine functioning, information usage, and HR.[98] A weaker link in any function generates a domino effect that frustrates business resilience.

During the COVID-19 disruption, some corporations demonstrated operational flexibility by finding new asset uses. Liquor manufacturers turned to hand sanitizer production. Electronics manufacturers produced thermal guns. Apparel companies manufactured personal protective gear. In Kenya, Bedi Investments reconfigured its production lines to produce surgical facemasks and PPE equipment, covering the Kenyan local demand and exporting to other countries.[99] Unilever used to make hand gel as a tiny fraction of its global business before COVID-19. However, when the company saw an opportunity for hand gel in the wake of COVID-19, it reconfigured some production lines to multiply the production of its brand gel, Lifebuoy, by almost a thousand times, making it one of the highest-distributed hand gels.[100] LVMH, the global brand maker of Dior and Givenchy, switched selected production lines from perfumes and cosmetics to hand sanitizers, covering a significant part of the French and European markets.[101] Airliners converted passenger planes into cargo to exploit the growing demand for perishable goods during lockdowns.[102] Some aviation companies diversified revenue streams, adapted to the changing market conditions, controlled costs, expanded routes, invested in technology, improved operational efficiency, and collaborated with the aviation community worldwide.[103]

Collaboration

Collaborative working relationship with external stakeholders is critical for organizational resilience during crises.[104] Collaboration increases an organization's capacity to spot, rally, and consolidate response resources in the wake of a disaster.[105] The collaboration of banks with Fintech companies enabled banks to expand online business operations.[106] During the COVID-19 pandemic, many SMEs established collaborative relationships to sustain operations. Some SMEs even managed to record profits.[107] For instance, collaboration with PPE manufacturers in China saw a Kenyan SME prosper during the pandemic by enabling a just-in-time supply chain network to a ready market, enjoying up to a 70 percent revenue increase when the global economy was in turmoil.[107]

POST-CRISIS RESILIENCE TRAITS

The post-crisis or crisis terminal stage is the period marking the end of a crisis. It is when we sigh in relief and declare the crisis "over." This period is also known as the normalcy period, which comes immediately in the aftermath of a crisis. But crises are cyclical in that it is just a matter of time before we experience another crisis. For argument's sake, let us assume an example of an armed assault on a peaceful gathering. Let us assume that the assault ended and the assailant was apprehended. The crisis does not end there. People mourn their loved ones for a long time, wounded persons receive treatment for various durations, and seriously injured people could spend the rest of their lives with a disability. Those who escaped unscathed may require post-traumatic counseling, children who lost their parents in the assault will live as orphans forever, and the agony and suffering from a brief crisis could last for years. People and organizations require specific qualities to cope with the aftermath of a crisis. These qualities include adaptability, recovery, learning, and transformation.

Adaptability

The short definition of adaptability is "a positive adjustment," and the extended definition is "deliberate choices and actions taken to deliver a unique mix of value to the market while keeping the organization abreast of changes within its ecosystem."[108] This book defines adaptability as "an evolving process to sustain existence in a dynamic environment." An example of adaptability is how traditional banks worldwide adapted to the informal SME segment by gradually expanding their market reach to the unbanked populations through strategy adjustments, self-reinvention, leveraging Fintech, and corporate restructuring.[49]

Adaptability in a dynamic environment requires adjustable resources, business-friendly corporate structures, reliable systems, flexible processes, and supportive culture. A weak link between these factors and adaptability becomes an unachievable dream. Adaptability is often faced with resistance due to entrenched corporate cultures that tend to resist change. To adapt to change, leaders must move decisively to lead the process and navigate the challenges; take a proactive approach to risk management and contingency planning; diversify their revenue streams; and improve inter-stakeholder relationships.

Recovery

Recovery is the restoration of functionality after a disruption.[109] Not all organizations can weather disruption. Recovery is a painful process that could result in financial losses, change of size, staff retrenchment, loss of market share, engagement of external stakeholders, dilution of ownership, and potential legal liabilities.[110] During the recovery phase, organizations require a clear management strategy to build resilience, diversify revenue streams, invest in relationships, increase spending on training, recapture lost clientele through tailored promotion policies, enhance product and service delivery, and improve communication.

Relearning

Post-crisis relearning is an indispensable trait of organizations that survive crises. Knowledge means acquiring and successfully implementing new skills to adapt to changing conditions.[111] Most disruptive events contain an element of novelty due either to a lack of prior experience in dealing with them or because they unfold in strange ways. Take the case of COVID-19, for instance. As remote working became the only practical alternative for business continuity, many organizations had to learn how to manage virtual teams and train staff to work effectively from home. Relearning is about managing the crisis and building capacity for future events. After the Chelyabinsk meteor strike, NASA and the Russian Space Agency collaborated to develop capabilities to detect and divert Near-Earth Objects to prevent a repeat of the Chelyabinsk-type strike in the future.[112]

Investment in relearning requires significant financial resources and comes at a time of competing priorities in the recovery phase. Therefore, resilient organizations should not wait for the disaster to strike but rather embed all scenarios and eventualities in their risk-management framework. A remote crisis today may be at your doorstep tomorrow. The enterprise risk management framework should be flexible and regularly updated to model new industry-level emergencies. Leaders should ask: What if a crisis like that happened to our organization? Are we prepared? If not, how do we prepare? What if a terrorist attack took place in our neighborhood? What if we had to recall our flagship product? What if another pandemic struck? What if innovative technology disrupted our core business? What if our anchor customer found a cheaper alternative? What if we lost our leading supplier? Such questions are activated by scenario thinking, embedded in strategic foresight, and integrated into the DNA of risk-aware organizations.

Scenario thinking triggers policy responses to what-if questions that enhance an organization's strategic resilience. Strategic foresight enables leadership to discount future risks into their current risk management policies. Risk diversification is a policy response anchored in resilience thinking. Mr. Njoroge, a Kenyan entrepreneur running an event management outfit and a lab, told me, "You can't rely on one income stream."[107] It is a simple risk management principle that one should not put all eggs in the same basket. When COVID-19 caused Mr. Njoroge's event management business to shut down, he sustained income from the lab business. He initiated awareness campaigns and networking sessions by bringing together small business owners to share their experiences using virtual platforms. Unintentionally, he revived his event management business and integrated it with his lab business.

Transformation

Transformation is the ability to transform positively after a crisis.[113] It enables firms to bounce forward into new possibilities. Transformation is an organization-wide tool. It covers product, service, system, and business model transformation and market outreach.[114] A study of US and European firms found strong evidence that innovative transformation was a leading cause for their ability to withstand supply chain disruptions.[115] Similar results have been documented in the Netherlands, where small firms' survivability has been established as a direct outcome of their ability to transform using innovation and technology.[116]

PRE-CRISIS RESILIENCE TRAITS

Assessing an organization's resilience at the pre-crisis stage is sometimes challenging because the crisis is not yet in full swing, so it cannot provide a real test. In manufacturing, industries test new products on surrogate environments to mimic real-life situations. Vehicles are pretested for endurance, safety, and impact survival. Guns are tested for caliber penetration and sustenance. Planes are tested for extreme weather endurance and maneuverability. Medicines are tested on surrogate environments. In all these cases, there is always a level of deviation between the surrogate environment and real life. Organizations benefit from hindsight of prior crises to prepare for future incidents. Agility, situational alertness, and robustness become critical at the pre-crisis stage.

Agility

Agility refers to a swift response to disruption. Agility is measured by a combination of direction and speed. Direction is the mission, and speed is the thrust or momentum. Direction comes first, followed by speed. An organization that runs without direction will hit a wall somewhere. An organization that maintains direction without motion will be pointed in the right direction but remain still and quickly overtaken. In a crisis, organizations do not enjoy the luxury of time. In a crisis, direction plus speed—not might—becomes the game-changer.[117] Decisions and actions must be taken with the available resources and while on the move. Nothing is perfect. In a crisis, one must prioritize completion over perfection. Perfection is irrelevant, even if achieved. When the COVID-19 pandemic hit in late 2019, only businesses that swiftly developed response plans managed to survive disruption.[49] The ones who waited around for a perfect solution struggled much more in the long run.

Agile organizations establish a common purpose and clear communication channels across hierarchies. They set up operational and administrative structures that support seamless decision-making. They create coherent team-networking patterns and set transparent reporting, accountability, and collaboration. They develop a culture of mutual support and team empowerment and invest in practical solutions that enable team members to perform their duties without hiccups.[118]

Agile organizations boast of a coherent operational culture. They move forward as one block with no issues. Decisions taken at the top management level pass smoothly to various functions and departments. Members of coherent organizations speak the same corporate language, observe unwritten etiquette, communicate with heart, react with logic, argue with reason, differ with respect, and walk with pride! Corporate swagger! Right? A coherent organization is like a military corps unit. While the military cherishes order and obedience, coherent organizations relish allegiance to the common cause.

Agile organizations preserve operational traditions even when they transform into large multinationals. Agile organizations grow organically because they provide a healthy environment for career progression. Leaders who grow in the organization's ranks have better knowledge of its strengths, weaknesses, and cultures. They are potentially more likely to stick with the organization. Agile organizations are better equipped to handle crises by proactively repositioning to exploit opportunities arising from crisis-induced shocks.[119]

Situational Alertness

Pre-crisis situational alertness enables organizations to anticipate, sense, and monitor developments in their operating environments for timely actions and to avert future liabilities. They monitor internal and external conditions to identify threats and sniff out opportunities.[120] Recall the fund manager in Chapter One? That was a classic demonstration of pre-crisis situational alertness. The fund manager in a

US housing market closed a credit default swap operation just before the financial tsunami, saving his company more than 60 million dollars. Situational alertness is a personal intelligence attribute some people possess naturally, but it can also be developed through training.

Robustness

Pre-crisis robustness is a resilience trait that aims to intentionally integrate organizational resilience strategy into organizational policies, structures, culture, and strategic plans.[121] At least half of the war against disruption is won with preparedness.[122] Empirical studies show that the 2008 financial crisis had a more severe impact on corporations that were caught unprepared than those with well-defined resilience strategies already in place when the crisis hit.[123] Robustness increases the chances of organizational survival and sets them up to seize latent and manifest market opportunities.[121]

Self-Cascading Reflections

Organizations are continually in the middle of a disruption, out of a disruption, or preparing for a disruption. As we reflect on this statement, let us take a moment to reflect on an experience we had with a crisis, whether at the individual or organizational level and ask ourselves the following questions:

- What were the most outstanding within-crisis resilience traits we manifested or observed?

- Can we identify all the within-crisis resilience enablers and hindrances?
- What were the most outstanding post-crisis resilience traits we manifested or observed?
- Can we identify all the post-crisis resilience enablers and hindrances?
- What were the most outstanding pre-crisis resilience traits we manifested or observed?
- Can we identify all the pre-crisis resilience enablers and hindrances?

Bend Your Mind!

Have you ever thought of how resilient Planet Earth is? Planet Earth is 197 million square miles (510 million square kilometers). Its circumference is 15,444 square miles (40,000 square kilometers). The size of the observable universe is estimated at 95 billion light years. Planet Earth's ratio to the observable universe's size is comparable to a grain of sand in a desert. On this grain of sand, we happily revel. We celebrate the New Year, Saint Valentine's Day, International Women's Day, International Men's Day, Children's Day, Labor Day, World Kidney Day, April Fools' Day, Earth Day, World Environment Day, World Humanist Day, International Friendship Day, International Lefthanders Day, Global Love Day, Memorial Day, National Heroes' Day, Pirate's Day, International Day of Peace, Piano Day, World AIDS Day, and Human Rights Day, among countless more. We are continually in celebratory mode. So why do we fight?

The nine nuclear countries spent \$83 billion on nuclear weapons development in 2021 alone.[124] The development of nuclear weapons is based on a naïve paradigm: deterring the adversary. It is known that a full-scale nuclear conflict will spare no one, including the orchestrator. Starting a nuclear war is tantamount to committing suicide.

Earth has enough food to feed every mouth and enough wealth to make everyone rich. The Earth is built to last. It has been there for billions of years when we were nonexistent. It cannot collapse in our lifetime. We will not be there to bid it farewell by the time it retires. The Earth sneezes, sobs, warms, ventilates, and protests. When it sneezes, we are blown away; when it weeps, we are washed away; when it warms, we burn; when it ventilates, we are drowned; and when it revolts, we are gone. By preserving the environment, we are doing a favor to ourselves, not to Earth. The current literature on the environment is misleading because it typifies us as doing a favor for the Earth, but in truth, by preserving the environment, we are doing a favor for humanity. If we do not preserve the environment, we will go, and the Earth will stay. Extinct reptiles will recapture their habitats. They are the aborigines of the Earth. We are not. We replaced them.

Chapter Four
RESILIENCE RESOURCE IDENTIFICATION

> Fear and hope are twin sides of our image. One is egotistic inside, and the other is flattery outside. If we overcome self-inflicted fear, we are left with one concern to focus on: hope.

Springboard

The wheels of life must keep turning. We can observe this truth plainly in the California desert, home to a curious amalgam of animals, all struggling to survive. One chilly night, a kangaroo rat stepped out into the eerie darkness in search of food, oblivious of a camouflaging rattlesnake with sinister motives peeping uncomfortably close beneath a pile of sand.[125] Then it happened. The attack was swift! The rattlesnake lurched forward with a deadly stunt that had the rodent right into its jaws. But if the snake thought its sniper-like precision was a sure bet, another thing was coming. In the blink of an eye, the kangaroo rat sprung high above the ground and—spinning in midair like an infuriated martial artist—unleashed a stunning pair of flying kicks that jolted the snake on its neck, dispatching the now bewildered snake down the opposite direction with an undignified thud.[126] It was a Bruce Lee-style karate knockout. The whole encounter was over in a matter of milliseconds. Before the poor rattlesnake could regain balance, the kangaroo rat had long vanished into thin air.

National Geographic captured the epic battle using night vision cameras and replayed it in slow motion. The statistics in the video footage were even more astonishing: "in 23 attempted lunges by the snakes, only one hit a rat—and it managed to survive."[126] That is about a 100 percent survival rate. As if that is not enough humiliation to the snake community, in another instance, a disdainful kangaroo rat—in what looked like a calculated offensive—deliberately kicked a nasty mouthful of dirt right into an unsuspecting rattlesnake's throat, causing the snake to cough, curse, and swear uncontrollably. And, in an unrelated episode, a magnanimous kangaroo rat is seen patiently drumming its foot to shoo away an unwelcome snake that had trespassed into its backyard.

Kangaroo rats are members of the Heteromyidae family, and the particular one just animated is called *Dipodomys Californicus*, a no-nonsense kangaroo rat that won't entertain affront from infidel snakes.[127] According to the narration in the video footage, kangaroo rats can sense the slightest air pressure change from predators in a matter of a millisecond. That is plenty of time for it to activate a lightning bolt response. This is because they have audio receptors with a sensitivity power 90 times that of humans, thanks to substantial hollow spaces in their skulls that naturally amplify sound.[126] In the blink of an eye, kangaroo rats spring into high-octane, adrenaline-fueled action, powered by disproportionately huge hind legs with thick tendons and large muscles that eject them from danger like a demented missile. Serpentine tails enable kangaroo rats to dodge out of predators' jaws, regain balance in mid-air, deliver a counter-offensive swipe, and successfully land on the ground unhurt before making an insane dash into the horizon.[128] Blink, and you won't know what hit you. Kangaroo rats are ordinary rodents with extraordinary resilience resources that have since earned them the nickname "Ninja Rats." Like Ninja Rats, resilient organizations possess unique resources distinguishing them from their non-resilient counterparts. This chapter provides a taxonomy of such resilience resources.

Within the organizational resilience discourse, attention has been drawn to slack or buffer resources, which refer to the bundles of resources a firm possesses more than is required to sustain their normal daily activities.[129] This book uses "slack" and "buffer" interchangeably to refer to reserve or contingent reserves that companies currently don't utilize and therefore set aside for eventualities. Slack or buffer resources empower firms to anticipate and sense current conditions, allocate people and resources flexibly, and change and adapt in an innovative and timely manner to address any adversity.[130] Resource endowment provides the necessary cushion for firms to experiment with their business models and positively impact enterprise sustainability.[131] Some scholars have underscored the role of such resources as they provide organizations with the capacity to absorb disruptive shocks.[132] In this respect, there are three overarching organizational resilience resource classifications: financial buffer, reputational buffer, and human capital buffer.[133]

FINANCIAL BUFFER

A financial buffer positively impacts firm resilience by insulating the firm's core operations from external shocks.[134] Financial buffer comprises three sub-dimensions: available buffer, recoverable buffer, and potential buffer. A solid financial buffer is critical to organizational resilience during a crisis because it allows an organization to weather unexpected events and sustain operations during those events. A financial buffer includes sufficient cash reserve, a diversified revenue stream, and a solid financial plan. Reviewing and assessing financial performance can also help identify and address potential vulnerabilities.

Available Financial Buffer

Available financial buffer refers to liquid assets that can be called up and deployed at short notice. The available financial buffer is the most flexible and readily available resource an organization can use to respond to disruptive shocks.[135] An organization can absorb shocks by tapping into excess capital, capital reserves, or liquidity.[133] Cash is cash. Cash is king. Cash is the lifeblood of a business, whether at hand or in the bank. Every business needs cash to operate. Cash defines an organization's survival.[136] Businesses with little or no cash tend to be philosophic about it. It does not work. It is either cash or no cash. Cash equivalents include redeemable or discountable instruments and money market funds. Most of an organization's dealings with its environment are transactional, and cash is the medium of exchange in a transactional relationship. Available financial buffer almost exclusively offers insulation against disruptive events.[137] If you have cash, you can negotiate while imposing your terms. If you have no cash, you negotiate and pray for the mercy of the counterparty.

Deliberate deployment of a business's resources to build a cash buffer is critical for resilience. Cash acts as a shock absorber that enables stability and continuity when faced with disruptions. Findings on the role of prudential policy in buffering COVID-19 losses in Switzerland's financial industry signify that a business's resilience capacity is contingent on maintaining an available financial buffer.[137] The business model post-COVID-19 highlights the financial buffer's central role in ensuring business resilience through bank solvency.[138] An available financial buffer is an organization's first defense line in distress. It not only buffers functioning but also facilitates opportunities.[139] It helps organizations during a disruption by promoting the organization's innovativeness and improvisation and providing a cushion against the liquidity tensions caused by the disruptions in operating performance.[135]

Available financial buffer is signified by the extent of liquidity, whereby organizations with low liquidity become vulnerable to disruptive shocks.[135] During the 2008 financial recession, Berkshire Hathaway was one of the companies that survived and thrived. The "cash is king" slogan has informed the investment philosophy of Chief Executive Officer (CEO) Warren Buffet for decades. Warren Buffet likes to reserve at least $20 billion on the company's balance sheet to respond to adversity. When the 2008 global recession struck, the large cash balance not only insulated Berkshire from the associated market turmoil but also enabled it to exploit the weaknesses of other market players. Warren Buffet is driven by the belief that a disruptive shock will happen eventually, thus always keeps a large cash balance in readiness. His investment philosophy is to be ready to take advantage of market downturns because when that happens, the market offers valuable assets at throwaway prices.[136]

The significance of available buffer to organizational resilience is not just for exploiting market opportunities or absorbing financial shocks but for presenting financial capability that cushions an organization's psychological capital. Money is not the solution to all problems, but it solves many problems. This is an ecclesiastical truth understood by Warren Buffet. An empirical study found that financial conditions and the risk of depression are related: the better the liquidity position of an organization, the lower the risk of depression to individual organizational members, and the better the clarity of mind to strategize and implement a response.[140] What is true for corporations is true for individuals. Financial security makes you sleep faster, sleep better, and wake up with energy; it is a fact.

Recoverable Financial Buffer

Recoverable financial buffer refers to uncommitted resources that need some effort to transform into an available buffer, such as inventories, accounts receivables, and other freehold assets that an organization can convert into cash or use to sustain itself in times of distress.

The utility of a recoverable buffer depends on its ability to be deployed and the inherent costs involved in the deployment process. For example, companies can use prepayments to obtain cash discounts, and stock can be sold out through clearance sales. Companies that possess highly marketable properties can also liquidate them.

In an article I co-authored on the banking sector resilience in Kenya, the recoverable buffer was a salient theme identified in the document content analysis. Loan loss provision and loan restructuring represented the two ways banks achieved this.[49] For instance, one of the banks identified provisioning for bad loans and growing loans and advances as key recoverable buffers since they can recall these when needed to boost liquidity. Another example is the divestment of non-strategic marketable assets. While reeling from the aftershocks of the 2008 financial crisis, Barclays Bank sold its stakes in Africa after more than a century of presence to shore up its core capital ratio.[141]

Potential Financial Buffer

The potential financial buffer includes accessible but unused credit lines or equity that an organization can tap into when the need arises to level out business cycle shocks and disturbances.[142] Credit lines are essential liquidity sources that enabled firms to survive the COVID-19 pandemic. Like available and recoverable buffers, the potential buffer is essential for organizational sustainability because it allows the breathing space needed to respond to disruptions rapidly and sustainably.[143] The availability of a potential buffer depends on a multiplicity of factors, most notably the level of balance sheet leverage, measured as the level of debt. The COVID-19 pandemic, for instance, triggered a worldwide upsurge in businesses' drawdown of credit lines with their banks as a precautionary measure to shore up liquidity needed to survive the pandemic.[144]

Potential buffer is inversely related to debt load: the higher the debt load, the lower the potential buffer—and the opposite is also true. The implication is that resilient organizations maintain a debt load that is light enough to attract external financing during periods of financial distress. When the COVID-19 pandemic hit, many large firms found themselves with low cash buffers and rushed to the debt market "to secure funds for covering operational expenses, and possibly buttress their cash buffers."[145] For instance, following the COVID-19 pandemic, Starbucks, an iconic global chain of coffee shops, doubled its debt load to bolster its financial buffer.[146]

The SME sector, which does not enjoy ready access to debt compared to large corporations, devised creative ways to create and access potential buffers during the COVID-19 global economic crisis. In Kenya, SMEs negotiated flexible rent-payment arrangements with their landlords; others rescheduled their loans and obtained extended grace periods, overdraft facilities, and trade credits.[107] Resilient organizations also survived through access to grant funding, which can become another source of potential buffer. The United States Small Business Administration (SBA) is an example of such a funding source, as it offers small business grants to spur entrepreneurship. Apex Entertainment, LLC, a movie theater business severely hit by the COVID-19 disruption, managed to recover after receiving grant funding from the SBA, which, according to the owner, "provided the much-needed financial stability to keep the company in business."[147] Similar interventions exist in many countries worldwide. However, it takes the initiative, preparedness, and effort to access this source of financial buffer due to, among others, limitedness to targeted sectors, stringent application requirements, and bureaucracies involved.

REPUTATIONAL BUFFER

Resilient organizations embed, create, preserve, and enhance reputational assets as part of their resilience strategies. Corporate reputation is a goodwill asset an organization builds over time and is handy during a crisis. The currency of reputation is trust, which is gained when the organization fulfills stakeholders' expectations.[148] A company's reputation is critical for resilience in crisis because it can significantly impact its ability to attract and retain customers, create partnerships, and attract new investors. A positive reputation can help a company to weather a crisis by providing a buffer of goodwill and trust. In 1982, a crisis occurred when Tylenol, one of Johnson & Johnson's top-selling products, was tampered with, and cyanide was found in some capsules, leading to several deaths. The company pulled all Tylenol products off the shelves, regardless of the cost, and offered refunds to customers.[149] Johnson & Johnson's reputation for honesty, integrity, and customer safety helped it regain consumer trust quickly. A negative reputation can exacerbate the impact of a crisis. The Deepwater Horizon oil spill in 2010, which caused significant environmental damage and harm to the local economy, was blamed on BP's handling of the incident, resulting in a share price drop and a negative impact on the company's reputation and public trust.[150]

Reputation management is an important aspect of crisis management and should be integrated into a company's resilience strategy. This book recommends regular monitoring and assessing corporate reputation, implementing measures to protect and enhance it, and establishing a crisis communication plan to effectively address any issues that may arise. Currently, most corporations manage reputation aspects under corporate and communication services. While this practice is sound—as it places corporate image and reputation aspects under the direct responsibility of leadership—it may not be sufficient, particularly for companies that operate in industries prone to third-party liability. Considering the potential impact of reputation issues on corporations, such as the cases of the Flint water crisis, the Grenfell Tower fire, the United Airlines crisis handling, the Volkswagen emissions scandal, and the NFL handling of the Ray Rice domestic violence case, one would argue that it may be worthwhile for corporations to consider having a function dedicated to corporate reputation within the C-suite apparatus, such as Chief Corporate Image Officer or Chief Corporate Reputation Officer. Public relations functions in some organizations perform part of corporate reputation aspects, but it is critical to elevate the function to a C-suite level.

Financial Reputation Buffer

Financial reputation is creditworthiness, the foundation upon which potential buffer is built. When distressed, organizations with a positive financial reputation survive shocks through preferential access to financial lifelines. Financial reputation is built through maintaining good credit history, consistent positive returns, and demonstrated ability to meet contractual obligations. Analysis of the content of 10,000 Australian firms' annual reports over 17 years established that a firm's capacity to sustain above-average performance over time was enhanced by its superior financial reputation, suggesting that financial reputation acted as a resilience lever.[151]

A good financial reputation also acts as a lever in negotiating trade and credit terms. A study of 7,000 firms from 58 countries found that companies with poor credit reputations experienced trade credit rationing during the COVID-19 pandemic, signifying that financial reputation predicted access to trade credit volume in times of crisis.[152] Similarly, resilient firms overcame a widespread credit crunch during the 2008–2009 global financial recession by using trade credit to supplement operating capital, allowing them to remain in business as non-resilient firms collapsed.[153]

Relational Reputation Buffer

Relational reputation is the quality of an organization's relationship with its key stakeholders—employees, suppliers, customers, bankers, community, and government. It refers to how well or poorly an organization is known to treat people.[154] Resilient organizations respectfully handle stakeholder relationships regardless of expected returns. A cordial relationship with stakeholders is vital to sustaining the organization through good and challenging times. Relationships are bidirectional: the give-and-take principle governs them. Organizations that build rapport with stakeholders on mutual respect will find this rapport handy on a rainy day.

Relational reputation is the basis of stakeholder collaboration, cooperation, and goodwill. Research across multi-sectoral firms in Central and South America, Africa, South Asia, and the Middle East established that reputation is a meta-resource that allows firms to build transactional confidence during crises and uncertainty.[155] Relational reputation attracts and retains talent and fosters employee loyalty even in disruption. It boosts employee morale and inspires them to go the extra mile, particularly during hard times. [152] An examination of the manufacturing sector in India established that HR commitment contributes to organizational agility, adaptability, and alignment.[156] During the 2008–2009 recession, Ford Motor Corporation faced prospects of collapse, which it averted partly due to sacrifices of its staff. Ford staff took the company's financial woes as their problem and willfully forfeited some benefits for recovery. The media quoted the vice president as crediting the company's resilience to its good relationship with its workforce.[157]

A relational reputation makes customers more willing to stick around even during challenging times. Organizations that relate well with their customers increase customer loyalty and patronage to soften blows from business downturns. [152] I once had a conversation with a Kenyan veteran banker, and he told me this about relational reputation:

We know banks that have gone through crises here in the country, but because their customer service was on top, most of their clients still went back even after the bank rebranded and started using other names and went through a very difficult phase. I speak from experience because I am also their customer. Most of us felt they treated us as kings and queens. We resolved that we are here to stay. We know this is a rebranding. I think what you do during the good times enables your customers to stay with you even during the rough waters. This is something that organizations need to cultivate and be intentional about.[49]

An excellent relational reputation makes customers feel secure in buying the organization's products and services. A favorable relational reputation is especially crucial for the survival of SMEs. Most SMEs operate from rented premises and outsource ancillary services to avoid unnecessary overheads. The owner of a small business in Nairobi told me that at the peak of the COVID-19 pandemic, he could no longer afford the rent and decided to relocate. Relocation is not an easy choice because it means losing customers—essentially, he had to start all over. However, due to his excellent working relationship with the landlord, the landlord reduced his monthly rent by 30 percent and offered him a flexible tenancy plan to pay up to three months in arrears.[107]

Product Reputation Buffer

Product reputation goes hand in hand with relational reputation. Product reputation is the consumer attitudes and perceptions about the quality of the products and services offered by an organization. The attitudes and perceptions can either be positive or negative. Customers want to feel they can depend on the product to serve its purpose. Products of impeccable quality are more likely to sustain demand irrespective of market realities.

A study of the impact of resources on the performance of 223 Malaysian listed firms that survived the 2008 economic meltdown found that intangible resources positively and significantly impacted their performance.[158] During the COVID-19 pandemic, as companies that produced substandard face masks counted their losses and risked closure following a crackdown by governments, those with a quality reputation thrived on government support and consumer choice. In 2020, the Ontario government awarded two million dollars to Smart Safe Science, a Canadian technology company reputed for making medical-grade masks.[159]

Company reputation is driven by its product brand, customer service, packaging, innovation, beautification, and the company's citizenship responsibility. Apple's reputation for producing high-quality products helped the company retain customer loyalty during the 2008–2009 global financial crisis. Patagonia, an outdoor clothing company, is known for being environmentally friendly and socially responsible. This helped the company retain customer loyalty during the COVID-19 pandemic. Ford has a reputation for building reliable vehicles, and this reputation helped the company keep customer loyalty throughout its history. Brand reputation is also evident in Coca-Cola, Unilever, McDonald's, and many others.

Citizenship Reputation Buffer

Citizenship reputation is a long-term investment that a corporation derives from integrating fundamental societal values in its business practices.[160] Integrating societal values into an organization's objectives and operations secures its sustainability simply because the organization's life depends on the host community's quality of life and the health of its ecosystem. Societal sustainability is, therefore, a cornerstone of the organization's resilience metrics.[152]

Kenya's Equity Bank transformed from a small loss-making building society in the 1990s to one of East Africa's largest and most profitable banks. During its transformative journey, the bank positioned itself as a microfinance institution with a social mission: to deepen financial access to Kenya's economically marginalized population. This earned the corporation a reputation for uplifting the community's quality of life.[161] Equity Bank leveraged its societal reputation to draw investors and funders worldwide, including International Finance Corporation, European Investment Bank, United Nations Development Program, and Department for International Development.[162]

Being considerate of the public reaction saves the corporation's image in challenging times. During the 2008 global recession, Starbucks recorded historically inferior performance and faced aggressive competition, consumer activism, and a highly contagious social media space with active bloggers ready to spin storylines. The company's president activated a turnaround strategy that entailed closing thousands of coffee shops across the US. The move attracted negative publicity from mainstream and online media. A leaked memo entered the blogosphere, and a gossip website spread it like wildfire. Phones at Starbucks started ringing from reporters asking for comment and requesting an interview with the president.[163]

Through that dark season, Starbucks was unfazed. The company focused on two of its most critical assets: employees and customers. It prioritized personal connections and enduring relationships over growth, and employees were treated as partners in every sense of the word, from full healthcare benefits to stock options to flexible working hours. Starbucks created an ambiance of community where every employee felt like being the owner of the business and every customer was treated with respect.[164] Once again, in 2016, a viral video depicting the company as racist sparked public protests that turned into a crisis, which the company managed to contain due to its solid reputation with the local communities.[165] Starbucks survived these crises by investing in its public image.

HUMAN CAPITAL BUFFER

Human capital buffer is an emerging concept in HR literature. It constitutes a mix of leadership capabilities and psychological capital, enabling organizations to lead with resilience—inspiring resilience in others—during challenging times. It includes the critical mass of people at various levels in the hierarchy who are adequately trained and prepared to take charge when called to duty. People with leadership capabilities who lack psychological capital do not constitute an organization's reliable human capital buffer. Psychological capital (PsyCap) is one of the most significant forms of human capital. PsyCap is a hidden trait only activated in challenging situations. The often touted "person of the moment" manages an everyday professional life and fulfills their daily routines but switches into a superperson when the organization faces challenges. PsyCap is a diamond deposit that lies untapped in the depths of an organization and is mined out when the need arises. People with PsyCap are not always known to every person in the organization but are well-known to the leadership. They are called to perform specific tasks, which they perform with unmatched success. They then return calmly to their ranks after accomplishment. Those people possess rich PsyCap.

PsyCap comprises self-efficacy, hope, optimism, and resilience. Self-efficacy motivates people to perform, hope drives multiple solution pathways around constraints, optimism challenges counterproductive beliefs, and resilience prevents setbacks.[166] PsyCap people are typically calm, humble, introverted, and highly focused. In corporate meetings, they usually listen more than speak. They often live in the shadow and do not like showing off. They are corporate Ninjas. Because an organization is as resilient as its members, resilient organizations intentionally create and build a sense of each of these four PsyCap facets in its human capital stock.[167]

Self-Cascading Reflections

Resource endowment provides the necessary cushion for organizations to experiment with their business models and positively impact enterprise sustainability. As we reflect on this statement, let us take a moment to ponder our own personal or organizational resources. Let us now reflect on the following questions:

- What financial buffers are currently available to us, and how sufficient are they to cushion our organization—or us—from future shocks?
- What practical lessons can we draw from Warren Buffet's investment philosophy?
- What does the deployability of our recoverable buffer—or the recoverable buffer of our organization—look like?
- As we assess our debt load (or that of our organization), what practical steps can we take to reduce high debt load to acceptable levels?
- Resilient organizations embed, create, preserve, and enhance reputational assets as part of their resilience strategies. How can our organization achieve this?
- Does our organization possess a critical mass of people at various levels in the hierarchy who are adequately trained and prepared to take charge when called to duty?

- What practical steps can be taken to increase the numbers?

Bend Your Mind!

Our PsyCap is the greatest driver of our personal resilience, indeed. Lao-Tze said, "Watch your thoughts; they become words. Watch your words; they become actions. Watch your actions; they become habits. Watch your habits; they become character. Watch your character; it becomes your destiny."

How many sides does an image have? A person's image has two sides: the inward side and the outward side. Who sees the outward side? It is everyone else. Who sees the inward side? It is the owner of the image. A full image is perceived from all directions. A distorted image is seen from one side. We spend time refining the outward lens of our image. It is natural. We all want to look good, feel good, and be perceived as perfect. What about our perception of our own selves?

Most of our actions are either driven by fear or hope. Fear of being depicted as ridiculous is a hope to maintain steady status. Fear of losing status is a desire to remain the center of attention. Pushing to grow the outer side of the image while ignoring the inner side expands the detachment between the two sides of the image over time. The outer layer keeps growing, and the inner layer keeps shrinking.

One intriguing observation is how some people master the art of camouflaging, appearing as perfect fits when they are internally none. With time, they master this art. However, the more they act, the more they believe in their lie. At a moment of stark reality, as the pressure gets unbearable, the glacier crumbles into the stifling air, causing the image to explode, throwing everything in the open air. Stories surround us of corporate leaders, politicians, dictators, and affluent persons ending their lives in prison, destitution, or rocked with scandals. Those people only cared about how people perceived them, but internally, they were villains.

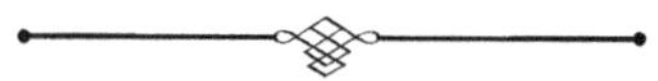

Chapter Five
RESILIENCE RESOURCES ORCHESTRATION

> Leaders do not readily bench your winning players for the loss of a game. Remember your PsyCap people and fend for your diamond reserves. Challenging times expose their DNA. They metastasize, with you or not, as they sense threat. But to hit that exocytotic moment, you ought not to have been one *off* them but one *of* them.

Springboard

n honor of Sir Richard Branson's epic balloon voyage…

A vessel entered a strong air-current zone several miles above sea level in the northern hemisphere. The pressure nearly shattered the vessel. Almost half of the vessel's fuel was lost, and one tank caught fire. Two occupants, the only ones in the vessel, managed to extinguish the fire and attempted to steady the vessel by discarding an empty fuel tank. The jettison attempt caused two other healthy tanks to drop. The subsequent weight loss uplifted the vessel to outer space across the Pacific at 200 mph (322 km/h). The occupants had two options: to recluse to the cabin and wait for their fate or to leverage the jetstream to dispatch them to some destiny. Both options were a huge gamble. They chose the second option, and the gamble paid off.

The hot air balloon, known as Virgin Otuska Pacific Flier, measuring 74,000 cubic meters, and designed and built by Thunder & Colt, landed Sir Richard Branson and Per Lindstrand safely hundreds of miles from their original landing spot. They broke the World Air Sports Federation record and entered the Guinness Book of Records.[168] Sir Richard Branson and Per Lindstrand orchestrated a safe landing through tough choices and within an extremely tight schedule. They had no time to think twice or plan on paper. They relied partially on instinct and luck and mostly on believing everything should be fine.

Like Sir Branson and Lindstrand, organizational leaders face choices that entail time-constrained orchestration of limited resources to sustain resilience. While resource differential is at times critical, it is not always the abundance of resources that makes a difference but how leaders can orchestrate those resources that set resilient organizations apart. This chapter punctuates resource orchestration with Branson's ventures and other exceptional accounts to unpack the concept of resilience resource orchestration and elucidate its dimensions with practical examples and case studies.

Resilience resource orchestration is derived from Information Technology Resource Orchestration. In IT, resource orchestration aims to improve workload recovery's reliability, speed, and granularity in cases of unplanned outages by automating disaster recovery processes while lowering disaster recovery exercising and operations costs.[169] This book borrows the concept of resource orchestration from information technology literature and proposes the resilience resource orchestration concept. In previous chapters, I argued that resources only foster resilience when infused with specific leadership actions that give resources an added impetus. Hence, resilience resource orchestration is the orchestration of resources that have been made resilient through deliberate leadership actions. Resilience resource orchestration illustrates how organizations can use available resources to build resilience. Resources are input factors deployed to create value.[170] With this expansive definition of resources, resilience becomes a resource that organizations orchestrate, bundle, and leverage to generate sustained corporate value.

Resource orchestration is a modern concept in management literature. It has been defined as "the deployment of firm resources effectively by structuring the portfolio of human and material resources at disposal, bundling the resources into capabilities, and leveraging those capabilities to create value."[69] Various frameworks and postulations have been put forward to give managers a mental model for strategizing resilience. The most notable are Dynamic Resource-Based View, Resource Orchestration View (ROV), and Dynamic Resource Orchestration Framework (DROF). [69] Whereas each addresses a set of variants that fills a specific gap, all three underscore the salient role of leadership in coordinating organizational resource deployment.

The distinctive features of resilience are agility, reframing, improvisation, collaboration, robustness, adaptability, recovery, learning, transformation, innovation, and diversification. These features are enabled by a unique mix of three input factors: financial, reputational, and human capital. Thus, the resilience input factors are enablers of resilience features. Hence, resilience resource orchestration is the use of resilience to orchestrate resources.[171] Organizations intentionally cultivate resilience, and resilience sustains organizations. Organizations and resilience are like trees and water. Trees help make rain through transpiration and photosynthesis—moisture originating from roots gathers on leaves, then evaporates into the atmosphere to condense into clouds, pouring rain back to Mother Earth to sustain trees and other life. In the same way, organizations create resilience, and resilience sustains organizations. It is like a payback from a long-term investment. Resilience is a long-term process that pays back for years ahead.

Resilience resource orchestration passes through three stages: structuring disposable resources, bundling them into intrinsic capabilities, and leveraging on the capabilities to create sustained value. Organizational leadership orchestrates resources. But leadership is a form of organizational resource. Leadership is a super resource because it can orchestrate other resources.[172] Let's begin by discussing resilience resource structuring.

RESILIENCE RESOURCE STRUCTURING

Resilience resource structuring conjures up the image of an organization beginning on a clean slate, such as a startup. However, resilience resource orchestration is more about restructuring as an adaptive response to the frequently changing micro- and macro-environments. It has been recognized as a method of revolutionary change that signifies the transfer from an existing to a new structure, enabling a higher degree of effectiveness and efficiency when it comes to managing business transactions, thus guaranteeing a better rate of survival and development of the company. [173] Thus, this book uses "structuring" and "restructuring" interchangeably to mean the same thing. Resilience resource structuring is the umbrella term for acquiring, accumulating, and divesting resources. These resources span human, financial, technological, and social resources that can be used to generate value. [174]

Human Capital Resource Structuring

Human capital structuring is a conscious leadership policy geared toward identifying, acquiring, and obtaining competencies from factor markets. [175] Competencies can either be outsourced or grown organically. Any organization's most critical competence cluster is the bundle that constitutes its C-suite. The C-suite market is competitive. Therefore, an organization that can build and retain a substantial C-suite is an organization that cares for its human capital. [69] Often, organizations that become casualties of disruption do so because of the low quality, inadequate quantity, and poor capability of members of the C-suite. The C-suite members are the colonels of the corporate army. They are the brigade commanders and the deciders of the corporate fate. When they separate from the organization, they leave with a contingent of highly performing and loyal staff. Hence, their separation has a compound effect on the organization.

Therefore, some organizations are eager to retain C-suite members on short-term contracts or as consultants, even as they retire or become less productive.

The second critical item in human capital structuring is its optimal distribution within the organization. Nowadays, most senior officers and members of the C-suite can befit most roles in an organization. The leadership's role is to orchestrate an optimal distribution of talents to increase their productivity and relevance to the organization.[176] For example, Safaricom Kenya was already performing well when the late CEO Bob Collymore took over leadership from Michael Joseph in 2010. Collymore instigated a management restructuring by merging some functions, collapsing others, and creating new functions. That sole transformation saw Safaricom soaring into the ranks of the up-and-coming companies in East Africa. Within a brief period after Collymore's advent, Safaricom became an $11 billion company, and its shares multiplied by 500 times.[177]

In stark contrast to Safaricom's success story, a former Kenyan banker whom I interviewed about sources of bank resilience told me a story of a local bank that failed the resilience test due to a lack of timely human capital restructuring. Here is what he said, and I hold the real names for confidentiality:

> *After failing to do the right thing, it became evident that this institution was going down. The Central Bank of Kenya…got involved from afar; the board got jogged a little, the management started shifting, people like [name of high-rank officer] went home. You*

can see a lack of succession planning and sole re-callings. …You find somebody like [name of high-rank officer] came in. He did not know about managing a bank, but because he was just lined up, he was the guy who took over. He again within that one year, just did the bank no good at all, and finally, they went for new blood which they got from [name of a local bank]. That guy came with new ideas, he went straight ahead and saw a loss-making side of the bank, and he said, 'No, that one I don't want.' Those are things that ought to have been done a long time ago.[49]

Human capital structuring also includes efforts to develop resources within the firm. This is mostly associated with learning and human capital development to increase firm-specific tacit knowledge.[178] Some companies, like Starbucks, even tried asking customers to leave so that learning could occur. Doors were closed at 5:30 p.m. across all its 7,100 stores countrywide in the US, as it was time to watch a short film demonstrating how to steam milk and pour espresso correctly. Within a few weeks, Starbucks's coffee scores rose, sparking excitement from customers and turning them into patrons.[164]

Financial Capital Resource Structuring

Financial structuring is a reorganization of a firm's capital structure to make the firm more financially sustainable in the face of changing operating conditions. Financial structuring is operationalized by altering equity, debt, and liquidity positions to make the financial obligations more manageable and generate a financial buffer. Desirable outcomes for any form of financial structuring include adequate cash flow, affordable funding sources, growth-friendly capital structure, low balance sheet leverage, good profit margins, and efficient capital deployment.[179] When businesses face operational challenges and prospects of failure, business owners are often advised to inject money into the business. However, injecting new money is not easy when a company is not performing satisfactorily. It means bringing new faces into the boardroom, borrowing at high premiums, or selling premium assets.

Companies that fail to bring in new equity or raise affordable debt often divest by shedding off firm-controlled resources, retrenching staff, selling non-core assets, selling under-utilized resources, or spinning off peripheral businesses.[180] Divesting has become one of the fairest means to resuscitate distressed businesses. Divesting shifts resources to more productive use but requires courageous decisions to shed burden assets and substitute low-productive assets with highly productive ones.

When considering divesting decisions, companies often prioritize the weakest link: staff retrenchment.[181] Most corporate restructuring experts believe achieving a turnaround without an initial period of planned retrenchment is rarely possible.[182] However, retrenchment is among the riskiest moves, often fraught with operational, ethical, and legal challenges. While a carefully planned and humanely implemented retrenchment scheme can work in favor of a company in distress, unthinking reactions can be catastrophic.

As the attempt of Sir Branson to retrench the empty fuel tank off his air balloon accidentally led to the loss of two healthy fuel tanks, staff retrenchment can sometimes worsen the company's situation by sending off the good guys and keeping in the bad ones. Amazingly, bad folks always find ways to stick around.

Most organizations hire outsiders to orchestrate staff retrenchment, but this is again a double-edged sword. Consultants rely on resumés and interviews that last for a few hours. But interviews and resumés do not tell the whole story, as they do not adequately assess attitudes and work culture, which are critical for distressed companies. Orchestrating staff retrenchment through ad-hoc internal committees is not an alternative option due to the risk of bias. Some organizations offer early retirement as a way of staff retrenchment. This is also a perilous strategy as it could lead to an uncontrollable exit. In May 2002, the Midlands State University of Zimbabwe faced a mass exodus of its 2,500 staff when it implemented a voluntary retrenchment scheme to shore up its sinking operations. Staff oversubscribed to the scheme, and nearly every employee opted out, citing demoralizing working conditions. The university readvertised for the vacant positions but failed to attract the targeted mass.[183]

Instead of resorting to staff retrenchment as an easy option, leaders can convert the organization into a crisis management beehive where every staff member fires all cylinders, works harder, is more innovative, and accepts some form of reduction in benefits. However, this will only be possible if staff members feel they are part of one family. It will be doable if they know they are making sacrifices for their future. It is attainable when employees feel they are masters of their destiny, working not for the payroll but for growth and a brighter, more secure future. Leaders should lead by example and apply pay cuts proportionate to earnings per head. Starbucks sailed through the 2008 financial crisis when every staff member felt that the company's problem was their problem and when they saw the leadership leading by example. Challenging times often bring out the true character of people. It may well be that those whose hearts are not in their work with the company will leave, on their own volition, to look for greener pastures. Do not fret—those folks would not have done any good for the company even if they remained.

Earnings retention is another suitable form of financial structuring. Retained earnings increase a firm's capital base and bolster its resilience.[184] Earnings retention increases available buffer through the capital reserve and lower leverage metrics to augment borrowing capacity and reduce the company's perceived credit riskiness. It is not unusual that a company like Berkshire Hathaway only paid dividends once during the 1960s.[185] Berkshire's rationale is simple: earnings retention, when efficiently redeployed, generates compound interest, has tax advantages from reinvested capital, and creates long-term shareholder value from a better stock valuation. But again, earnings retention is only possible if the company has earnings to retain in the first place. In most cases, companies in distress will have accumulated consecutive losses that erode their earnings by the time they have reached the edge. Let us investigate a perfect example of what ignoring financial structure can do to business. Nakumatt Holding was a store retailer family business that started operations in Kenya in 1978. Over the years, Nakumatt built a strong brand and expanded into East Africa. By 2017, the company had 6,500 employees, boasted 65 stores across five countries, and recorded $600 million in annual sales. In that same year, Nakumatt went bankrupt.[186] Nakumatt's troubles began as early as 2009 when it reported its first operating loss. However, because Nakumatt was then perceived as the sole household store of convenience in East Africa, the owners persisted in an expansion spree, opened multiple outlets in Uganda, Rwanda, and Tanzania, and planned to expand into West Africa.[186]

In 2013, Nakumatt was declared by a global credit rating agency as a high-risk enterprise, signaling that it was experiencing financial distress while overtrading. Owners again ignored the signs and continued expansion by tapping into their financial buffer. Through the following years, Nakumatt exhausted its entire financial buffer and got into the pockets of suppliers with delayed settlements and disputes over invoice values. As some suppliers and property owners moved to court, Nakumatt experienced a string of property confiscations and eviction notices, which shook the company and triggered austerity and turnaround measures very late in the game. By that time, the company's name was damaged beyond repair. By 2018, Nakumatt had only six stores operating out of 65 the previous year and had a debt book of $360 million.[186]

Technological Capital Resource Structuring

Technology is the most critical differentiator among peer organizations. Today, technology is a do-or-die for organizations. Technology integrates business sections, delivers timely value to customers, reduces the cost per operation unit, and increases productivity per head.[187] In 2000, Equity Bank installed its first core banking software, including Finacle, Oracle, and Hewlett-Packard hardware platforms. The system conferred the bank a large room to scale up its operations. The results were dramatic! Account opening took as little as five minutes, branch expenses dropped, and interconnection with other banking service solutions became seamless, leading to an agile response to demand for innovative products.[162] Demand for services kept soaring at an outstretched capacity rate, forcing management and staff to work late into the night to stabilize systems and rationalize operations. Equity Bank's share price traded at 183 shillings, up from 70 shillings, within a short time.[188]

Another example is the Commercial Bank of Africa acquisition by the National Industrial Credit Bank to leverage CBA's superior digital banking position.[189] The merger outcome saw unprecedented growth for the National Commercial Bank of Africa Group PLC. Also, Safaricom Kenya fully acquired the Mpesa brand through a joint venture with South Africa's Vodacom, setting the stage for an intelligent, cloud-based mobile banking platform.[190]

Social Capital Resource Structuring

Social capital is a term used to describe the value of social networks, norms, and trust that facilitate cooperation and coordination among individuals and groups. Organizations with social capital are more resilient to systemic shocks due to the positive externalities they generate through leveraging their social networking. Examples of social capital include common language and shared understanding, friendship groups, business networks, spiritual communities, volunteer organizations, social media, communities of practice, and family bonds.

In corporations, social capital is the quality of the relationships that a firm—and its executives and employees—have built with other stakeholders. Corporations that invest in social capital earn the trust of their stakeholders, thereby enhancing cooperation and potentially leading to better economic outcomes for the firm.[191] Social capital can contribute to a company's success by building a sense of shared values and mutual respect. It can help keep talented people in an organization by initiating them into its culture, allowing them to learn from others, and making them feel part of the whole. This can lead to better employee retention rates and a more productive workforce.

One way to build social capital is through the corporate social responsibility umbrella. This includes efforts to improve relationships with employees and the local communities where the firm operates and to protect the environment and human rights of people who live in those communities. [192] Organizations can develop social capital by building trust through transparency and authentic leadership, providing time and space for people to connect and have personal conversations, and establishing recognition and reward systems that support and reinforce collaboration. Companies can also invest in social capital by demonstrating a real commitment to retention and fostering cooperation.[193]

RESILIENCE RESOURCE BUNDLING

Resilience resource bundling maximizes value by generating new product and service capabilities through reconfiguring and combining existing resources and capacities, thus building unique and more valuable capabilities in a dynamic and volatile business environment.[187] Each capability a firm possesses is a unique combination of resources that allows it to take value-creating action for itself and its stakeholders.[194] Bundling aggregates resilience resources into capabilities and capitalizes on those capabilities to generate value for the organization.[194]

Stabilizing refers to extending the productive life of the organization's core material assets. Enriching enhances the productivity of an organization's core human assets through training and development. Pioneering is finding new uses for the material and human core assets. Sequentially, pioneering comes after stabilizing and enriching. The logic is simple: pioneering requires exceptional skills and capacities only attainable once the corporate has achieved perfection in its core business. Hence, once material asset output is refined through stabilizing and human asset output is refined through enriching, the organization will be poised for sustained resilience through pioneering.[194]

Resilient organizations intentionally and regularly make minor incremental improvements in existing capabilities, slightly alter a firm's mix of resources, make necessary investments in supporting and sustaining resources, and restore weakened resources through enriching and stabilizing.[175] They invest in core competencies and continuously endeavor to add productive value to a firm's resources. A veteran Kenyan banker I interviewed told me this about enrichment:

> *I would like to appreciate the bank where I was working because there was a lot of staff training. Staff were being trained to help us upskill ourselves, be at par with the world, and know how things are going. Basically, what I'm saying is trained our staff more and maintained the staff, the trained staff, so that they don't have to shift from one bank to another one. If the staff is moving, it means that the performance of the bank is affected in one way or another.*[49]

Creating new capabilities can sometimes be achieved by recombining unrelated resources, bundling new, complementary resources, and combining unique and valuable resources with existing ones. These processes help organizations orchestrate assets, build flexibility, and avoid core rigidities. Pioneering entails an element of innovation as it involves firms' constant search for new products, relationships, and markets to expand their scope and growth. Safaricom's Mpesa innovation is a perfect example of pioneering. The company capitalized on its mobile communication infrastructure and subscriber base to provide financial solutions, which is an unrelated product. Virgin's brand proliferation under Sir Branson is another perfect example of firms pioneering new frontiers by leveraging available capabilities. For example, if someone asks you to describe the link in all Virgin Group's subsidiaries in one word, that word would most likely be "pioneering."[195]

People often confuse pioneering with expansionary ventures. Pioneering is driven by leadership vision, while expansionary ventures are driven by market research and, in some cases, mere herd-style behavior and competitive spirit. In most cases, expansionary venturing fails because of embedded short-term tactics. The case of Nakumatt Holdings was a perfect example of expansionary venturing that led to the total collapse of the Group. Expansionary venturing is almost synonymous with corporate cannibalism. While cannibalism relapses business growth due to one product shifting market from another, expansionary venturing regresses growth by altering the geographical relevance of the business and pushing it to venture into unchartered waters with neither proper swimming skills nor reliable life vests.

RESILIENCE RESOURCE LEVERAGING

Resilience resource leveraging is the mobilization, coordination, and deployment of resilience resources. An organization can grow successfully through resilience resource leveraging by efficiently adjusting and implementing strategies in a turbulent environment. Once again, Safaricom's Mpesa represents one of the best examples of leveraging as it turned mobile handsets into personal bank gadgets. Equity Bank also exploited its mass-market base to introduce Equitel, a digital financial service, by issuing free SIM cards to its nearly nine million customers nationwide in 2014, making it Kenya's second leading mobile money transfer service after Safaricom's Mpesa.[188]

Whereas mobile money transfer services found a conducive environment, resilience resource leveraging is possible even in hostile conditions. Like how Sir Branson leveraged a hostile atmosphere to propel the balloon faster toward their intended destination, resilient organizations frame adversity as a resource to be exploited for maximum advantage. It is the same way liquor manufacturers leveraged their production capacity to manufacture and supply hand sanitizers to exploit the demand vacuum generated by the COVID-19 pandemic. It is the same way kangaroo rats mobilize, coordinate, and deploy their resilience resources to outsmart rattlesnake disruption. Resilience-oriented organizations leverage resilience resources to win their survival battles.

Self-Cascading Reflections

It is not always the abundance of resources that sets resilient organizations apart but how leaders orchestrate those resources. Safaricom's CEO, Bob Collymore, instigated a management restructuring by merging some functions, collapsing others, and creating new functions altogether. The company also capitalized on its mobile communication infrastructure and subscriber base to provide financial solutions, turning mobile handsets into personal bank gadgets. Equity Bank Kenya installed core banking software that conferred the bank a large room to scale up its operations. In the skies, Sir Branson leveraged a hostile atmosphere to propel the balloon toward their intended destination faster. On the ground, Sir Richard Branson pioneered new products and market frontiers by leveraging available capabilities. As we reflect on these cases, let us take a moment to consider the lessons we draw from these examples regarding resilience resource orchestration. Let us now reflect on the following questions:

- What resilience resource orchestration skills do we observe from these CEOs?
- What resources and capabilities can our organization leverage to respond to disruption?
- What sets successful organizations apart from the crowd in terms of resilience in their business environment?
- What would we do differently to set up our organization for prosperity, despite market realities?

Bend Your Mind!

If you ask kindergarteners to define jail, they may tell you it is where criminals are kept. So, all criminals are kept together, right? Jail is supposed to be a correctional facility, right? Now, how do we define a criminal? A crime is an act, meaning that a criminal is a criminal at the point of committing the crime and guilty after committing the crime. At the point a crime is committed, it is preventable through practical actions commensurate with the crime severity. After committing the crime, the criminal faces two liabilities: reversal of damage and prevention of future crime. Reversal of damage is the victim's right. Prevention of future crime is a societal right. Reversal of damage is assured through external justice delivered by the judiciary. Prevention of future crimes, however, requires a combination of external and internal justice. External justice is short-term, secondary, correctional, and institutional, such as imprisonment. Internal justice is long-term, primary, educational, and self-driven, such as repentance and resolve to maintain steadiness in life.

To develop internal justice, a person must persistently be within a conducive ambiance that creates incentives for internal change. The current incarceration system in most parts of the world creates an environment where a jailed person only sees fellow prisoners and prison wardens. Occasionally, priests, imams, and rabbis visit to talk about faith. That talk becomes like sport game fixtures. Prisons affiliated with churches, synagogues, and mosques might be subjected to more spiritual guidance. If prison wardens were trained psychiatrists, they could help maintain the psychological balance of the inmates. If large prisons were broken down into small community hostels, and each community was assigned a hostel to look after, prisoners could feel that society has not repulsed them. These steps could help to transform prisons into an environment for genuine self-correction. At the end of the day, prisoners are societal resources that can be orchestrated in a positive way. Let us let their positive deeds emerge as a genuine urge to say "thank you" to society for being accommodating and forgiving, not solely to impress prison wardens and management for potential commutation.

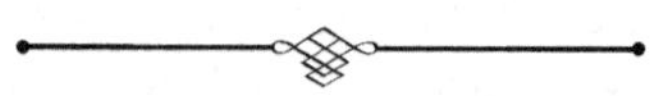

Chapter Six
RESILIENCE LEADERSHIP

> If there is one universal feature in most extinct organizations, it is their leaders' resistance to change.

Springboard

I n honor of Captain Sully's selfless self!

Tranquil waters lazily streamed down the behemoth River Hudson, occasionally meandering even lazier vessels, oblivious of an incident in the skies at a high altitude. A moment later, a massive splash shocked the nerves of the river, announcing the advent of an uninvited floater: Cactus 1549, with 155 lives aboard.[196] A brilliant, pale, graying-haired, erstwhile unknown Captain Chesley "Sully" Sullenberger orchestrated what has gone down in history as a rare act of selflessness. A head-on collision with reckless geese forced the pilot to activate a landing strategy known as the River Hudson Miracle. The story of Flight 1549 contains the same threads of leadership, training, planning, and preparation required for any corporation to be sufficiently able to respond when a crisis strikes.[197] Building on re-silience leadership as a deliberate emergent strategy—and drawing from the River Hudson Miracle lesson—this chapter focuses on the essential resilience leadership strategies required to navigate volatile situations.

DEFINITION OF RESILIENCE LEADERSHIP

Resilience leadership means reconfiguring the leadership ecosystem within the organization toward an optimal blend of leadership and management that collectively achieves its strategies.[198] Resilience leadership entails an organization's actions and policies to realize its transformational objectives. [199] It entails a blend of strategic, transactional, and trans-formational leadership infused with the flavor of strategic management.[200]

As John Maxwell said, "Everything rises and falls on leadership." The fall of Kodak has been attributed primar-ily to a lack of digital leadership strategy at the turn of the century. This period marked the beginning of the digital disruption era, which Kodak leadership failed to see because the leadership minds were imprisoned within the walls of the film culture. As the first company to introduce digital cameras, Kodak had created a tide on which they failed to ride.[201] Emirates Airlines, a barely five-year-old airline flying through turbulent headwinds during the early 1990s Gulf war, took a heretical move against the industry trend. Emirates increased its coverage to the region when all other major airliners cut back or grounded flights to the warzone. This was an incredible move that defied conventional strate-gic management thinking.[202] Operating amid a conflict in which air operations played a preeminent role, the airspace conditions over the Middle East were perilous. Yet, this decision saw the company continue to post profits and expand while its competitors recorded historic losses. Emirates became the fastest-growing airline and the only one that emerged unscathed by the global financial crisis, beating many industry giants.[202] The company's performance is attributed to its resilience leadership strategies.

Resilience leadership is a recent concept that emerged from mainstream leadership theory's inability to predict persistent organizational failure across various environments. It marks a shift in the emphasis of leadership literature from the social attributes of the construct to the behavioral attributes.[203] Conceptually, resilience leadership is anchored upon several parameters that coalesce around thematic characteristics, making an optimal mix of the lead-manage continuity. A synthesis of resilience leadership identifies five fundamental elements: leadership direction, leadership quality, leadership capability, leadership adequacy, and personal resilience intelligence. These elements portray profiles that leaders must possess to lead an organization resiliently.

LEADERSHIP DIRECTION

Resilient organizations have a clear direction where leaders know where they want to go and how they will get to where they want to go. Crises impose a change of course and destination. Therefore, vision clarity and path traceability generate ecosystem comfort and stakeholder support to the leadership to forge ahead with bold actions. Often, in moments of crisis, a split-second decision can make the difference between survival and demise. Unclear choice paths, multiple confusing options with high risks, and uncertain consequences typically characterize such choices.[79] Nonetheless, the choices must be made. The US Airways Flight 1549 pilot had to make the potentially catastrophic decision to land on the River Hudson. And he did. He made two critical announcements with existential implications: "We're gonna be in the Hudson…brace for impact."[96] There was no luxury of time to consult. This was, of course, an extraordinary circumstance. But then again, the frequent systemic events of the 21st century are just as exceptional. The point of resilience direction leadership is that in times of crisis, leaders need to be clear about where they want to take the organization to give its members a sense of direction. A clear sense of direction helps people to face the difficulties and uncertainties involved in the process.[204] Leadership direction is a function of the organization's vision, mission, and values.

Organization's Vision

Vision is a mental image of a desirable future that inspires positive action.[205] In classical strategic management, the scope of value an organization creates, the market it serves, its priorities, and its future outlook are expressed in its mission and vision.[206] A well-assimilated vision carries an organization through time and space.[207] Resilient organizations possess clear and compelling visions.[208] Dr. Martin Luther King Jr.'s vision statement, captured in his "I Have a Dream" speech, was a great manifestation of the magical power of the vision.[209] A compelling vision speaks to the mission statement, and the two continually reinforce each other in ideal circumstances.

Organization's Mission

The organization's mission is the conduit through which its vision is housed, nurtured, and conducted to foster its values and achieve its objectives. A statement of mission explains why an organization exists. It addresses the question, why are we here?[210] More often than not, times of great adversity push people to question their existence. This is because traumatic events activate in people a search for meaning in a bid to cope, as meaning gives them a reason to continue living and persevere through difficult situations.[211] Thus, a clear and compelling mission provides meaning and becomes a coping source and an energizer. It gives followers an identity, purpose, and direction in times of chaos and confusion.[212] Like their vision statements, resilient organizations craft mission statements that strongly connect to the hearts and minds of their stakeholders. Mission statements pregnant with meaning strike a chord with its members. Such mission statements give members of the organization a reason to continue their membership and inculcate in them a fighting spirit.

Organization's Values

Suppose we symbolize an organization as a living being. Values constitute the soul, psychology, emotions, and feelings; mission represents physical prowess, muscles, and torso; and vision represents the brain, mind, and reason. Challenging times often present a litmus test to an organization's purported values.[213] Indeed, resilient organizations are so because they consistently demonstrate that their values are critical to them. Core values contribute to resilience when leaders become resilient role models "by adhering to the organization's core values and using personal narratives of overcoming adversity and achieving success to motivate team members."[214] However, role-modeling core values is a necessary, but not sufficient condition for lasting organizational resilience. An organization's members must share those values. Value misalignment is a risk factor in the organizational resilience equation. Shared values and common goals are foundational to organizational adaptiveness.[215] Therefore, organizational strength is a function of shared values, just like other elements of resilience leadership strategies.[216] Resilient organizations embed preparedness with mission, vision, and values that form their common identity and set them apart in the marketplace.[121]

Value alignment is a question of integrity and ethics. The ethical climate in an organization represents the salient ingredients of resilience leadership strategies that contribute to the realization and sustenance of organizational resilience. While constituting one of the necessary conditions for a successful resilience leadership strategy, an organization's ethics precedes all other strategy ingredients during a crisis.[217] Empirical evidence based on terrorist events in Oslo and civil war in Libya demonstrates that in highly volatile contexts, the substance of strategy and leadership changes from fixed formalities of hierarchical levels to a dynamic interaction where ethics become one of the most critical dimensions that drive, define, and differentiate resilient organizations from non-resilient ones.[218]

LEADERSHIP QUALITY

An organization's resilience posture is as good as the quality of leaders upon whom the ultimate responsibility of the organization's resilience is entrusted. I must define leadership quality first to apprehend this fundamental element of resilience leadership. This book's preferred definition of quality is "fitness for emerging purposes." This definition aligns with the overarching concept of resilience leadership as a deliberate emergent strategy. Leadership quality measures the extent to which those in crucial positions possess what it takes to steer the organization through expected and unexpected events. Leaders sustain relevance to their organization when they remain helpful in changing conditions.

Talent is the spine of leadership quality. Talent represents a highly skilled and gifted workforce with abundant competencies and capabilities, including the capability to face unexpected new situations, the desire and motivation to learn and apply knowledge in new ways, and the judgment to take the right course of action with agility and laser precision.[219] In essence, talented leaders are evolutionary and revolutionary at the same time.[220] Today's operating environment requires talented leaders who can skillfully navigate an organization through chronic and acute disruptions while harnessing opportunities to sustainably deliver stakeholders' prosperity with minimal or zero internal drama. Talent pool development cannot be achieved solely by prayer and well wishes. It is a creation and preservation by an intentional process achieved over time through sound talent management policies. It is the timely attraction, development, and retention of mission-critical talent.

As an organization's mission gives meaning to its members in times of tribulation, a talent pool is created by attracting the right talent. In the Law of Attraction, the like-minded attracts the like-minded. Thus, an essential first step in attracting the right talent is creating an image of a conducive environment that attracts that talent. That image is created through senior managers' strategic intent and actions, which infect the entire organization through contagion. After making a conducive environment for talent to thrive, the next step in talent pool creation is to deliberately scout people with a mix of resilience traits and potential at both the personal and professional level or a track record of success in creating value during challenging conditions.

Success in talent acquisition is subject to market forces, including supply and demand, in relation to internal organizational constraints, which may have a moderating effect on aspirations that must be reckoned with. The bottom line, however, is that at every layer of market power, any organization can still find labor with reasonable levels of talent to deliver under the circumstances.

Once attracted, the talent must still be developed. Empirical research that links employee training and development to organizational resilience has previously demonstrated talent repository as a resilience leadership strategy.[221] Even if the right talent has been attracted, the highly novel environmental realities mean that training and development will always be necessary to prepare the acquired talent for emergent roles. The reality confronting organizations is that well-trained and developed talent become more attractive in the labor market. Therefore, organizations must still compete to retain them. Innovative organizations lock in talent using service contracts and other reward management strategies such as employee share-ownership schemes. Yet even then, some of these traditional methods of talent retention do not necessarily appeal to today's generation of workers. For instance, research suggests that Generation Z workers—the youngest entrants into today's workplace—are more intrinsically than extrinsically motivated. In other words, they are energized by self-determination and autonomy and cherish pleasure and excitement over material gain.[222] Resilient organizations demonstrate resilience even to such generational change dynamics by devising creative ways to engage them. Perhaps, making workplaces more interactive and relaxed and linking them to a social environment could make workplaces more attractive to Generation Z.

LEADERSHIP CAPABILITY

Leadership capability is a function of alertness, adaptability, and creativity—the core of personal and organizational resilience.

Situational Alertness

Situational alertness is about vigilance to potential threats and opportunities that may have strategic implications for the organization. This often calls for systems thinkers as system thinkers are inherently able to join the dots between complex adaptive systems even when the complex adaptive systems relentlessly mutate. Perplexing challenges of the contemporary world have led to the proposition that systems thinking may hold the key to the lasting survival of humanity. Systems thinkers look at the bigger picture, take an ecosystem view, consider multiple perspectives by framing and reframing them in new ways, examine how system parts relate, search for root causes, and challenge paradigms.[223]

In today's fast-paced and ever-changing business landscape, anticipating and responding to potential threats and opportunities is crucial for corporate resilience. Alertness is one of the critical traits that organizations should cultivate in their leaders. This means being vigilant to potential risks and opportunities that may have strategic implications for the organization. For example, several corporations in Latin America and other geographies were able to pivot their operations in response to the COVID-19 pandemic quickly. [224] These companies could use their systems thinking capability to anticipate the shift to online shopping and remote working and quickly adapt their operations to meet the changing needs of their customers.

On the other hand, the lack of leadership alertness can have devastating consequences for organizations. One example is the way that the government of Venezuela failed to anticipate and respond to the 2019 economic crisis.[225] Despite clear signs of impending economic turmoil, the government was unable to implement necessary reforms, and as a result, the country's economy spiraled out of control. Millions of Venezuelans were plunged into poverty and faced shortages of necessities like food and medicine. [225] Considering the preceding, leaders must continually strive to cultivate alertness in their organization by nurturing a culture of open communication and creating an environment where employees feel comfortable speaking up and sharing their concerns. They must foster a learning culture by encouraging employees to invest continuously in their growth.

Adaptability

Adaptability is the single most central requirement for resilience leadership. Adaptability is simply about having an open mindset and willingness to learn and adjust to new possibilities. Adaptability enables leaders and teams to prepare for adversity and navigate through sensemaking; supportive coaching; clarifying goals and processes; building team confidence and capacity to improvise and reframe; and increasing psychological safety by speaking and acting appreciatively, leading by example, and debriefing team members.[226] The opposite of leadership adaptability is resistance to change. If there is one universal feature in most extinct organizations, it is their leaders' resistance to change. Resistance to change by the managers at Kodak brought the giant organization down. Similar incidences have been reported worldwide, including in Kenya, where interviews with ex-bankers revealed that an attitude of resistance to change undermined the resilience of some banks, leading to their inevitable acquisition.[51] In contrast, adaptive leaders build resilient organizations because they are more vigilant and keener to prepare for disruption—and even lead through it.

In Kenya, competitive disruptions forced banks to adapt by expanding their market reach to the unbanked populations. Some banks adjusted their strategy to reflect the circumstances; others reinvented themselves by embracing technology, and others started restructuring. A Kenyan banker I interviewed told me this:

> *To survive, definitely you had to change. The bank was now able to reach the unbanked—who had completely been forgotten—and also was able to relax the stringent requirements of opening an account. Now, all those things had to be relaxed.*[49]

Adaptability also manifests in the reorganization of business operations for the sake of business continuity, as reflected in the statement from an annual report of a Kenyan bank that went through turmoil but managed to navigate disruption:

> *We responded with intentionality to the pandemic ensuring that employees and customers were protected, shareholder value preserved, and communities supported. This included repayment holidays, fee waivers and loan restructuring for customers enabling them to weather the economic downturn in 2020. In a bid to protect the health of our customers, we have redirected them to mobile banking and enhanced contactless payments.*[49]

The arguments corroborate the findings of a study by Turgeon, who investigated leadership skills and competencies in a post-crisis organization and found that organizational resilience was the outcome of a demonstration of adaptability. This implies that an organization's adaptability depends on its leadership's adaptive capability.[227] Similarly, several vehicle manufacturing industries have adapted to the changing automotive industry by investing in new technologies, such as hybrid and electric cars, allowing them to mitigate the impact of rising fuel prices and stricter emissions regulations.[228]

Innovativeness

High-quality leaders exhibit various resilience qualities, including creativity, innovativeness, and risk-taking. Creativity is the ability to invent, devise, conceive, formulate, or design. Creative leaders have mastered the art of design thinking and can understand their environment, challenge beliefs, redefine problems, and innovate solutions. [229] Passionately creative people have an innate drive to bring innovations for fun. They draw excitement from taking innovation to a new level and disrupting the status quo. They are unafraid to reform or transform existing capabilities into uniquely new models with unintended, big-bang, disruptive consequences. An example is Angry Birds Classic, an online game developed by the Finnish video game developer Rovio Entertainments that attracted over a million downloads in the first few hours of release and hit 12 million downloads in less than a year.[230] It is the first online game to hit one billion downloads, which it managed in three years. Organizations must carefully study the creative mindset behind Angry Birds and other similar successes. The way Rovio Entertainment did it through rare talent nurturing, others can do it, too. Resilient organizations attract such rare talent by creating an environment conducive for them to thrive.

LEADERSHIP ADEQUACY

The last dimension of resilience leadership is leadership adequacy. As the name suggests, leadership adequacy is about numbers—the critical mass of leaders in the organization that can collectively navigate the organization through times of distress. Leadership is not the exclusive preserve of the C-suite of resilient organizations. In these organizations, leadership means positive influence. Resilient organizations recognize that constant change is the norm and are fully alive to the realization that times of change call for more leadership than management capability at nearly every level of the organizational hierarchy.[231] They know that people in leadership positions become handy during crises. The COVID-19 crisis spotlighted the critical need for talented leaders. In episodes of disruption, organizations look up to leaders who rise to the occasion in the face of existential threats and work tirelessly to navigate the disruption and lead organizations to safer shores.[232]

Leader Count

Leader count is the number of leadership positions commensurate with the organization's size and activity. Resilient organizations develop a pipeline of leaders at all levels of the hierarchy. They also create excellent and complementary positions of authority with the readiness to fill vacancies at short notice and have the discretion, resources, and protocol to take charge of the situation when the conditions warrant it. At no point or level do such organizations experience a leadership vacuum because movement across and up the next level of the hierarchy is almost automatic. HR monitors the leader counts to ensure deviations are always within the acceptable ratio.

Leader Seniority

Leader seniority is indicated by position, years of experience, education levels, and continuous development. Organizations that take their resilience seriously have the right mix of capabilities at very senior positions.[233] There is no one-size-fits-all when it comes to the optimal leadership mix, as this largely depends on the nature and requirements of each organization. However, there are generally accepted industry thresholds that the leadership in each organization can consider as guiding principles.[233]

Leader Education

Building organizational resilience requires the right number of people with the desired education to be in place at any time. A key focus of this is resilience education through continuous resilience development programs. The proper mix of skills development is worked into such programs commensurate with their role and mental capacity within the organization. For example, safety and issue management training may be more appropriate at lower levels, while systems thinking, scenario analysis, and strategic foresight may be more relevant higher up the organizational hierarchy.

PERSONAL LEADERSHIP INTELLIGENCE

Personal leadership intelligence comprises five core traits: adversity intelligence, practical intelligence, social intelligence, emotional intelligence, and spiritual intelligence, collectively referred to in this book as APSES core intelligence traits. An apse is part of a building that sticks out from one end, is usually semicircular, has an arched roof, and is often richly decorated, especially in Gothic churches. Apses are common in places of worship. From inside the building, the apse is where the spiritual leader stands to preach to the followers. In churches, apses are where all the faithful are called to focus their attention during a sermon or prayer.[234] In mosques, apses are where the Imam stands to preach and lead the congregation in prayer. Hence, it symbolizes a north star that guides followers to the right path. APSES is a term coined in this book to refer to the five human qualities that collectively make a transcendently resilient person-leader. Like the apses of spiritual structures, the five APSES represent the directional compass that fosters human resilience at times of hardship.

Adversity Intelligence

There is consensus that a positive attitude toward adversity is the right attitude, which has led to the emergence of adversity intelligence. *Adversity intelligence* measures how effectively individuals process responses to tragedies and is an omnibus indicator of an individual's perceived ability to prevail over life's misfortunes. Research conducted on a sample size of 507 women employees of commercial banks in India indicates that "individuals with low adversity quotient score tend to recover from adversities at a slow pace or enter into stress and depression, while those with high adversity quotient score have positive fortitude, recover fast, perform better by maintaining their delight, vigor, and vitality."[235] Adversity profiling is thus becoming a necessary emergent deliberate HR strategy for recruitment and selection, training, and development toward building a resilient organization.

Practical Intelligence

Practical intelligence is another resilience quality leadership that sets up an organization for long-lasting resilience. During adversity, practical intelligence equips organizational leaders with the ability to think positively, proactively, and promptly. It empowers leaders to take the lead in preparing their followers through supportive coaching, mission clarity, confidence building, and psychological safety. This is done by speaking and acting appreciatively, offering shared leadership, leading by example, and debriefing team members.[226] Of this rather extensive list, sensemaking, reframing, and improvising are perhaps among the most crucial practical intelligence competencies that should be found within an organization's pool of human capital. Disruptive events can be disorienting and thus require people who can maintain or quickly regain their sense of balance, craft a coherent forward game plan, and spearhead its implementation. Such people have a unique ability to see and seize the underlying advantage and have a knack for quickly reframing misfortune as an opportunity—often because they think creatively. Contemporary organizations increasingly rely on such people because they have inimitable insight to improvise into the unknown.[236]

Social Intelligence

Social intelligence relates to behavioral aspects of resilience leadership strategies and denotes the competencies associated with human skills that foster a collegial working relationship with other organizational stakeholders.[237] Social intelligence includes effective communication and soft leadership.[238] Research on the nexus between these resilience leadership strategies dimensions and organizational resilience resides within the broader transformational leadership discourse.[217] This discourse centers on interpersonal communication skills and emotional intelligence, which foster social resilience.

When a Virgin train carrying 120 people crashed at a speed of more than 93 mph (150 km/h), every comment made by a visibly emotional Sir Richard Branson "had the effect of ensuring that Virgin maintained a good relationship with all its stakeholders: employees, customers, train engineers, track engineers, emergency service, victims, and the wider public."[239] That Branson cut short a family holiday, rushed to the crash scene, and declared the train driver a hero was a human touch that restored faith in humanity and neutered all potential public-relations backlash.[239] Social intelligence is not just a necessary tactical asset for damage control but extends to the more significant role of damage avoidance. Social intelligence capabilities enable an organization's defense systems to know sooner and prepare accordingly. Today, social intelligence has taken center stage in military strategy.[240] In corporations, social intelligence is critical for C-level executives and board members seeking the best possible basis for their decisions.[241]

Emotional Intelligence

Emotional intelligence is a key enabler of social intelligence and is crucial for organizational resilience through the individual resilience of employees. This is because emotional intelligence is essentially about the management of one's own emotions in favorable and productive ways.[242] People with a high emotional intelligence quotient are more psychologically resilient to adversarial life events.[243] Emotional intelligence has been worked into International Labor Organization's global framework on core skills for life and work in the 21st century.[244] It is a particularly fundamental facet of leadership effectiveness, as it has been established that leaders with high emotional intelligence "show greater adaptability to change and ambiguity."[245] For instance, high adaptability with strong links to emotional intelligence was found among surviving leaders of four companies housed at the World Trade Center during the 9/11 terror event.[246]

Social intelligence, emotional intelligence, and attitude are highly interrelated and mutually reinforcing. Attitude refers to a person's settled thinking, typically positive or negative. It is common knowledge that the effectiveness of leaders is affected by their attitude. It is also often said that one's attitude determines one's altitude. Staffing an organization with people of the right attitude is therefore important for resilience building. This is particularly critical for senior positions because accumulating leaders with the right attitude spreads a culture of positivity down and across the organization.

Spiritual Intelligence

A final and summative part of the five APSES core is spiritual intelligence. But what is a spirit? Psychology defines spirit as 'the search for ultimate meaning, purpose, and significance, to oneself, family, others, community, nature, and the sacred."[247] Spiritual intelligence is "the human capacity to ask questions about the ultimate meaning of life and the integrated relationship between us and the world in which we live."[248] The outward manifestations of spiritual intelligence are high levels of faith, moral purity, humility, meditation, and belief in and reverence for a transcendent being.[249] The significance of spiritual intelligence to organizational resilience is gaining much traction in business, thanks to empirical evidence linking spiritual capital to positive organizational adaptability.[250] For instance, spiritual intelligence has been found to reduce job stress and turnover intention among nurses.[251] Spiritual intelligence was a manifest feature of resilient organizations during the COVID-19 pandemic. In empirical research that Dr. Kilika, Dr. Gakenia, and I carried out in 2021 on the resilience of nonessential service SMEs in Nairobi, we found that the most resilient organizations exhibited faith-based practices such as religious fellowship, prayer, and encouragement. One entrepreneur told us that "spiritual connection was instrumental in keeping their sanity intact despite the disruption and was their best resource."[107] Like the other four elements in APSES, spiritual intelligence is an acquired ability and can be developed over time.

Self-Cascading Reflections

The "River Hudson Miracle" provides an inspiring example of resilience and leadership in crisis. The incident highlights the importance of preparation, teamwork, decision-making, and communication in high-pressure situations. It also demonstrates that disruptive events can be disorienting and thus require people who can maintain or quickly regain their sense of balance, craft a coherent, forward game plan, and spearhead its implementation. Let us take a moment to consider the qualities and skills Captain Sullenberger and First Officer Skiles demonstrated during the emergency landing on the River Hudson. Let us now reflect on the following questions:

- Which of these qualities are identifiable in our team, and which are not?
- How did the crew's preparation and training enable them to respond effectively to the crisis?
- Do we possess all or some of these traits?

- If not, how can we build them? What was the role of communication and teamwork in the successful emergency landing?
- Are we satisfied with the communication culture within our organization?
- What lessons can be learned from the crew's response to the crisis that can be applied to other high-pressure situations?
- How does our organization prepare its leaders and employees for crises like the River Hudson?

Bend Your Mind!

Leadership and management are two critical elements of organizational success. Although they may sometimes intersect, it is imperative to comprehend their fundamental differences. There is a trend in the corporate world toward valuing leaders over managers for several reasons.

Leadership entails inspiring, motivating, and directing followers toward a shared vision. Leaders concentrate on the bigger picture, cultivate a supportive and inclusive work atmosphere, and empower their subordinates to reach their full potential.[252] They foster a sense of community, drive innovation, and promote collaboration, resulting in a more efficient and committed workforce.[253] Conversely, managers maintain stability and control, utilizing established systems and procedures to run the organization as it has always been run.

Managers concentrate on outcomes and results rather than developing relationships and fostering a positive work culture. They are often perceived as rigid and inflexible, lacking the creative and visionary qualities that leaders bring to the table. This distinction between leaders and managers is reinforced in the literature on leadership and management. Leading scholars such as John Kotter, Peter Drucker, and Jim Collins have emphasized the significance of visionary leadership and its effect on organizational success.[254] On the other hand, management literature has also stressed the importance of control, efficiency, and structure in managing organizations.[254]

Several successful leaders have transformed organizations by inspiring and guiding their employees. Some examples in the corporate world include Steve Jobs of Apple, Oprah Winfrey of Harpo Productions, Jack Welch of General Electric, and Alan Mullaly of Ford. They all created a shared vision and inspired their employees to work toward a common goal, resulting in remarkable growth and success for their organizations. Generals George Washington, Napoleon Bonaparte, and Sun Tzu are renowned for their combat and military strategy planning leadership. Nelson Mandela and Abraham Lincoln left a lasting impact on their countries through their visionary leadership. Martin Luther King Jr. and Malala Yousafzai have inspired change through activism and advocacy. In sports, Vince Lombardi, Phil Jackson, and Alex Ferguson are known for their ability to lead and motivate their teams to victory. Mother Teresa, Bill Gates, and Mo Ibrahim have significantly impacted the nonprofit sector by inspiring and directing their organizations toward a common goal.

Visionary leaders lead by example, set standards for ethical and responsible behaviors, and encourage their followers to do the same. They create a positive and inclusive work culture and foster collaboration and innovation, resulting in a more engaged and motivated workforce. They adapt to change and steer organizations through challenging times, making them essential to organizational success in today's rapidly changing business environment.

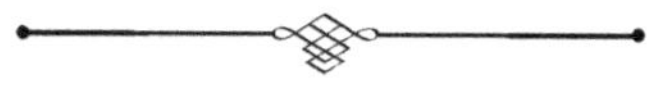

Chapter Seven
CORPORATE RESILIENCE

Toxicity is never exposed from a resumé; as malicious hearts escape institutional filters to zenith, organizations rot from the top and decompose downward, generating an ambiance of nonchalance and proliferating opportunism.

Springboard

The unsinkable that was once unthinkable!

The night was moonless. Deep in the Atlantic Ocean, a vast vessel navigated calm waters. Its occupants were exulted to be part of a historic feat of a lifetime. The ship was a breathtaking sight, the largest moving object ever made by humans—a magnificent work of craft. Targeting the opulent, the vessel reeked of luxury, with an interior décor and carvings that rivaled a palace.[255] The cost of building the vessel was conservatively estimated at ten million dollars—a fortune then and an outrageous cost by today's standards. The craft had 16 watertight compartments meant to stop the entire vessel from leaking in too much water and sinking if the body was breached. The engineering work that culminated in the boat was state-of-art.[256] It was a larger-than-life monstrosity of the 20th century and had design features that earned it a reputation as unsinkable.

An iceberg ahead on the vessel's path was not spotted until too late. What followed were desperate attempts to turn the behemoth—which was hurtling at frightful velocity—off the collision path, in vain.[257] The iceberg ripped its side with such force that the vessel began sinking, at an obtuse angle, fast into the deep waters. Before long, it had wholly submerged into the Atlantic Ocean, claiming the lives of 1,500 out of the more than 2,000 passengers on board. The unsinkable sank! More than 100 years later, the story of the Titanic is still being told.

Could the Titanic have been saved? This obvious question inspired various commissions of inquiry and commentaries for over a century. Investigations revealed that multiple red flags were ignored before and during the crisis, two of which were particularly significant.

Firstly, the aura around the vessel masked a mismatch between the number of passengers it could carry and the number of people its lifeboats could rescue. Because the transport company that owned the Titanic competed with its rivals for bragging rights over prestige, it was decided to load only 16 lifeboats onboard rather than the original 32 to convey an image of less clutter. It should also be mentioned that the actual project plan proposed 48 lifeboats—sufficient to accommodate enough legroom for comfort seekers—but this proposal was rejected by the company's chairperson, arguing that the ship was, in itself, a lifeboat.[258] The total capacity of the lifeboats was thus adequate for just over half of all the people on board.[259] This decision was made at the expense of safety. By the number of lifeboats versus the number of survivors, twice as many lives might have been saved if safety standards had not been compromised.

Secondly, before striking the iceberg, the Titanic had received at least six warning signs on that fateful night that it was perilously cruising deep inside an ice field.[260] Government investigators faulted the ship's captain for knowingly racing the vessel at full speed in a known ice field, again motivated by competition to break the existing record as the fastest ocean liner in shipbuilding history. The same arrogance and pride of its owners percolated down to its operators.[258] An inquiry report revealed that the operators neither discussed the matter of ice on its track nor increased their vigilance, even as other vessels doubled their alertness and stopped their engines. In one hearing, another ocean liner on the same route stopped due to ice and tried to warn the Titanic, to which the captain replied, "Shut up! I am busy!"[258]

This extraordinary story of the Titanic resembles the failures of many corporate giants throughout history. Like the unsinkable ship fallacy, the history of the enterprise world has been punctuated with the notion that certain corporations are "too big to fail." This doctrine stipulates that large corporations, especially in the financial sector, cannot be allowed to fail because of the potential adverse impact the failure may have on the rest of the sector and the economy at large.[261] When distressed, organizations leverage this fear to demand a bailout at taxpayers' expense. Too-big-to-sink and too-big-to-fail are analogous to the baby throwing her body in the air, knowing too well that her mother will never let her off-shoulder. It is a syndrome of adult corporations acting with a childish demeanor.

This chapter investigates corporate failures and successes and attempts to unpack potential answers to the questions raised in the first paragraph of the introduction to this book. The literature on corporate successes and failures is overcrowded to the extent that it makes any further contribution at best marginal in value. For this reason, I revisit corporate successes and failures with a new mindset to mine patterns and commonalities from raw cases that are well-known to the public.

SOURCES OF CORPORATES FAILURE

In the opening statement of this book, I asked: How do seemingly robust organizations fail without forewarning? Why and how does a blanket disruptive event affect organizations within homogeneous ecosystems variably? Why does a change of leadership bring about mixed results for corporations? Why are some organizations more efficient in creating value from comparable resources? Why do some corporations capitalize on disruption to grow while others divest and collapse? Why do some tiny businesses punch multiple times their weight while some larger ones crumble? What makes organizations fail, to begin with? And what makes them succeed? In this section, I attempt to explore some answers based on practical examples and case studies of corporate failures and successes worldwide.

One way to do so is to apply a simplistic deductive research method by analyzing selected underlying cases and establishing pattern commonalities across events. Corporate failure in all its forms and fancy names—distress, receivership, bankruptcy, protection, default—is one area that has been extensively researched. Corporate failure is loosely defined as a company's inability to achieve its financial and strategic goals.[262] There are various definitions, but failure to attain financial and strategic goals represents common ground since almost every company's purpose is to grow shareholder value as measured by its financial success in the marketplace.

There are several common causes of corporate failure; some are market-specific and industry-specific cases. Each corporate failure case is unique and cannot be replicated elsewhere. In each case of failure, there is a principal cause and other opportunistic causes that build upon the principal cause. Corporate failure does not necessarily mean corporate collapse or death. Companies can fail but metamorphose, resurrect, transform into another form, or even migrate into other businesses. Sometimes, company owners bring in new management to turn things around. They change names, enter mergers and acquisitions, or physically migrate to new geographies.

In this section, I review 24 cases of corporate failure. The review yields a broad classification of reasons for corporate failure into two categories: internal factors and external factors. This classification is generally in line with the findings of other empirical studies on corporate failure.[263]

I classify internal factors under three broad themes: leadership deficiency, vision myopia, and competency crisis. Leadership deficiency includes poor leadership, poor management judgment, and ethical insanity. Vision myopia includes a lack of innovation drive and poor corporate culture.

Competency crisis includes financial mismanagement and overtrading.

Likewise, I classify external factors into market dynamics, technology, and force majeure. Market dynamics include competition, regulatory environment, economic recessions, and political instability. Technology includes technological disruption and cybersecurity. Finally, force majeure includes supply chain disruptions and natural disasters. It is worth mentioning that this list of factors is non-exhaustive since various other factors may exist based on geographical context, industry dynamics, or historical reasons. These factors are discussed next.

Leadership Deficiency

As John Maxwell said, "Everything rises and falls on leadership."[264] Leadership deficiency is a principal cause and a common denominator in corporate failure. Leadership failure manifests in poor leadership judgment, leading to bad decisions. Poor leadership judgment leads to poor choices most of the time. Leadership competency transcends technical aspects to ethical, spiritual, situational, social, emotional, and personal integrity. A leader who lacks ethical integrity is not fit to lead. A leader who lacks emotional intelligence has no moral prowess to influence followers. A leader who lacks social awareness cannot cross-fertilize to generate stakeholder value. Leadership deficiency also manifests in the moral insanity of the whole or part of the top management team. When a corporation rots from the top, it decomposes all the way down because people imitate what their leaders preach and do. If corruption spreads throughout an organization, there is no way to cleanse it without amputation and chemotherapy, i.e., mass layoff. Leadership corruption generates an environment of nonchalance across the corporation and proliferates opportunistic behaviors from internal and external stakeholders to extract undue benefits, corrupting more people and spreading contagion. Therefore, leadership corruption is one corporate malady that must be dealt with, with the utmost firmness, by business owners and regulatory authorities.

Examples of corporate failure due to leadership deficiency include WorldCom, a telecommunications giant based in Clinton, Mississippi, which collapsed due to accounting fraud that involved inflating the company's earnings to maintain share value.[265] Similarly, HealthSouth, one of the largest corporations in Alabama, collapsed due to accounting malpractices.[266] Tyco International, a Princeton corporation, went under due to securities fraud and misappropriation.[267] Enron Corporation collapsed due to prolonged accounting misrepresentation. Enron's case was significant in the industry and went down in corporate history, as management maintained fake, healthy-looking accounts for a long time.[21] Livedoor, one of the most successful corporations in Japan, was implicated in securities and accounting fraud, leading to the arrest of its CEO.[268] The common thread amongst the above cases is leadership greed, lack of ethical standards, pursuing fame at any cost, and enrichment. Why do they do this? If you are a CEO or a CFO of a listed company (or just a company), you already have a secure financial return, can raise your family in decency, and have a good retirement package. You cannot live long enough to consume billions of dollars acquired illegally.

You will gather it for an inheritance, but your share will be a cursed name and tinted legacy. This might sound naïve to some people, but it is true: leaving behind a good name is a million times better than leaving behind a fortune.

Vision Myopia

Leadership with a lack of vision leads an organization unthinkingly into an impasse. In ordinary times, leadership myopia is never felt, as a corporation performs just within average. It is during trying moments when everybody looks up to leadership for a direction that leadership vision becomes a precious commodity. Leadership vision sanity positions an organization on a trajectory for long-term growth and sustainability. Leaders with vision see what is coming tomorrow and prepare their organizations to embrace change. Leadership vision manifests in how corporations innovate and mutate to remain relevant when times change. Companies lacking innovation become obsolete as competitors introduce new products or services, consumer tastes and demands change, and their core product loses relevance. Kodak is a classic example of a company beaten in its specialty as leadership vision was imprisoned to physical imaging.[269] Atari, once a household name in the gaming industry, failed to visualize what the video future looked like and was, therefore, slow to embrace change and compete with new products.[270]

Often, a lack of vision at the leadership level projects a loss of direction and purpose at the corporate level. When a corporation loses its compass, morale drops, employees lack the motivation to apply themselves to the limit, staff turnover increases, and corporations fail. In contrast, vision clarity injects morale and multiplies innovation. A senior officer at Equity Bank in Kenya told me that at the climax of Equity Bank's transformation, they could work late into the night and never feel exhausted. This was because the corporation was driving in a clear direction, heading to a common cause, and living for one goal: to outclass.

Competency Crisis

A competency crisis manifests in financial mismanagement, over-leveraging, overtrading, misallocating resources, or failing to invest in growth opportunities. Lehman Brothers' high-risk trading in subprime, mortgage-backed assets led to the company's collapse in 2008. This is a classic example of reckless trading by the company's executives. The company's failure had a ripple effect on the US market and the global economy and triggered a domino effect on the housing market, contributing to the global financial crisis of 2008.[271] American International Group (AIG) experienced a similar crisis by investing in risky assets and derivatives that lost value during the 2008 crisis. AIG received a bailout of $180 billion and had to reinstate its financials following a coverup of multibillion-dollar losses.[272] Nigerian Telecommunications Limited had a long history of financial struggles, poor management, and underinvestment. The company was privatized in 2001, but the privatization process was plagued by corruption and mismanagement. In 2016, the Nigerian government took over the company's management and filed for bankruptcy in 2018.[273] In 2014, Banco Espirito Santo Angola, a Portuguese bank subsidiary, revealed a hole in its balance sheet of $1.4 billion. The bank's management was found to have been involved in insider lending, leading to its collapse and significant losses for depositors.[274]

Companies that take on too much debt and leverage their balance sheets face difficulties paying their debts and eventually fail. Daewoo collapsed in 1999 after racking up $50 billion in debt.[275] Daewoo was a South Korean conglomerate active in various industries, such as automobiles, electronics, and shipbuilding. The company was founded in 1967 and quickly grew to become one of the largest companies in South Korea. However, in the late 1990s, it had taken on significant debt and faced financial difficulties. This led to a bailout and restructuring of the company, but ultimately it was unable to recover and was forced to declare bankruptcy in 1999.[276]

Market Dynamics

Market dynamics include competitive pressures, regulatory requirements, economic downturns and recessions, and political instability. Market factors usually corroborate and intertwine, making it difficult to isolate or pinpoint a specific market factor as a principal cause of corporate failure. For instance, regulatory requirements could affect the demand or supply of specific goods and services, leading to competitive pressure from alternative suppliers of substitutive products. Companies face intense competition from other businesses that offer comparable products or services.

Companies that cannot keep up with changing market conditions and consumer preferences face difficulties and eventual failure. Blackberry failed to anticipate the rapid rise of smartphone competitors, such as Apple and Samsung, and the shift from physical keyboards to touch screens. The company was slow to adapt to these changes and failed to stay ahead of the curve regarding technology and product innovation.[277] Blackberry left behind fond memories, and that was all. Other similar examples of corporations that collapsed or failed due to inability to match market speed include the British MG Rover Group, the American store chain Kmart, the Brazilian aviation company Varig, the South Korean shipping company Hanjin, the American medical service provider HealthSouth, the US retail giant Sears, and the Indian steel manufacturer Essar Steel.[278]

Technological Obsolescence

Companies that fail to adapt to modern technologies or changes in consumer preferences face difficulties and eventually die. For example, the rise of e-commerce has had a significant impact on brick-and-mortar retailers. I have recounted numerous examples of corporations that exited the market due to the inability to transform and adopt new ways of doing things. Borders, a major book retailer, faced difficulties due to the shift to digital books. Borders' management was slow to invest in e-commerce and digital technology, leading to the company's decline and eventual bankruptcy in 2011.[279] Technology risk also includes cyber-attacks, which most corporations do not take seriously. For instance, Equifax, a primary provider of consumer credit reporting services, suffered a significant cybersecurity breach in 2017 that resulted in the theft of sensitive information of millions of consumers. Equifax's management faced criticism for how it handled the breach and the company's inadequate cybersecurity measures, leading to significant financial losses and damage to its reputation.[280]

Force Majeure

Corporations fail due to various reasons that are not under their control. Supply chain disruptions and natural disasters are often quoted as two significant casualties of force majeure. Supply chain disruption happens due to strikes, port closures, wars, sanctions, hurricanes, wildfires, and other events that impact the availability of materials and products. The earthquake in Japan in 2011 and the ensuing tsunami had a significant impact on many companies in the electronics industry, as key suppliers in Japan were disrupted and unable to provide components to manufacturers worldwide.[281] Companies such as IBM and Hitachi faced significant supply chain disruptions due to the disaster. Similarly, Hurricane Katrina impacted many companies in the US Gulf Coast region, causing disruptions to operations and significant damage to facilities and equipment.[282]

Lessons from Corporate Failures

The woes of failing companies feature a toxic mix of environmental volatility and internal weaknesses. However, it can be construed that the internal issues were more pronounced, with the spotlight centering on corporate governance failures. Whereas environmental disruptions trigger the demise of once large and successful corporations, ecological forces are not necessarily to blame since industry peers thrive in the same volatile and unpredictable conditions. The greatest danger in all the corporations that failed, to use the words of Jeff Bezos, is the failure to evolve. And the singular latent theme in the collapse of large corporations is poor resilience leadership strategy (the total of resilience direction, quality, adequacy, and capability leadership). As Peter Drucker said, "Work productivity is not the workers' responsibility, but the managers."[283] The outward manifestation of this lacuna in large corporations that fail is poor corporate governance. Poor corporate governance is primarily responsible for the lack of financial prudence, resistance to change, complacency, leadership wrangles, lack of accountability, adoption of unsustainable business models, and overreliance on beliefs that fail to anticipate or recognize change.

CORPORATE SUCCESS DRIVERS

Like corporate failure, corporate success is multifaceted and contextual. A recipe for success in one corporation is challenging to replicate in another because of the multidimensional aspects of success: leadership, ecosystem, environment, market, regulatory thresholds, staff composition, resource availability, etc. Nevertheless, salient pointers of success can be borrowed to inform turnaround strategies in comparable ecosystems. In this section, I adopt the same extractive method of reviewing the cases of corporate success and deducting commonalities that I categorize into generic corporate success drivers. Based on a quick review of 15 cases of corporate success, I conclude that corporate success is driven by corporate vision steadfastness, consumer loyalty, self-reinvention, innovative growth, panoramic integration, and prudent expansion. Corporate success drivers are discussed next.

Corporate Vision Steadfastness

An unclouded vision is essential for corporate success as it provides direction and purpose for an organization. Without a vision, companies lack a roadmap for where they want to go and what they want to achieve, leading to aimless wandering and missed opportunities. On the other hand, organizations that have a well-articulated and ambitious vision are more likely to inspire and motivate employees, attract and retain customers, and create a strong brand identity. A vision realized and brought to life can drive innovation, growth, and profitability and help companies stand out in a crowded and competitive market. The common aspect in vision-driven corporations is transformation, growth, and value creation for shareholders and customers. Vision is entangled with resilience leadership strategies. Resilience leadership strategies are a tool to translate the vision into actionable milestones.

The vision effect is a lookback effect. In other words, vision impact can only be felt ex-post. Because vision-derived value is only realized ex-post, the journey toward its realization requires much courage due to resistance from traditional ecosystem components that want to keep the status quo for fear of detachment from the mother capsule. Detachment is a critical stage before any form of transformation. Like a newborn must be detached from the umbilical cord to transit into a new life outside the womb, corporations need the courage to detach from the old ways of doing things to explore and discover new growth frontiers. Because detachment often involves laboring and is marred by uncertainty, it usually sounds logical and appealing to keep what one has at hand and play safe. However, keeping the acquired gains and playing safe is an exact manifestation of a myopic vision because motion is bidirectional, and leadership controls only one part. If corporate leadership decides to play safe and consolidate historic gains, market dynamics shift, and the business loses its reason to exist. That is what happened to Kodak, Commodore, and Olympia.

Consumer Loyalty

Consumer loyalty is the cornerstone of corporate success in today's fast-paced and highly competitive business environment. With so many options available to consumers, retaining their loyalty and keeping them engaged is critical for any corporation that wishes to establish a strong and sustainable market presence. Achieving and maintaining consumer loyalty is a complex process that involves understanding the needs and preferences of customers, providing high-quality products and services, and building long-lasting relationships based on trust and mutual benefit. This ensures customer retention and helps organizations increase lifetime value, foster brand loyalty and word-of-mouth marketing, and drive business growth and profitability.

The story of the rise, fall, and second rise of Apple Corporation is intricately intertwined with Steve Jobs. Apple was founded in the 1970s in the garage of the house of Steve

Jobs's parents. The company quickly gained traction and achieved high growth in producing personal computers and related accessories. In 1980, Apple was listed, experienced a meteoric rise in share price, and earned a place in Fortune 500. Apple continued to record success before beginning to lose market share to Microsoft.[284] A series of events, including mergers and acquisitions, saw Jobs return to Apple in 1996. Under Jobs's leadership, Apple launched a series of successful innovations, the most notable being the iPod, followed by the introduction of the iTunes store. While Jobs rested eternally in 2011, Apple continued to soar the skies of success, guided by a robust corporate culture, brand loyalty, and good succession planning.[284] Like Apple being associated with product reliability, many other corporations in various sectors developed and consistently maintained brand identities that earned them market reputation and consumer loyalty. Samsung Electronics is famed for innovative technology, DHL for fast and reliable services, Oman Air for high-quality and personalized passenger services, and Shoprite for affordable products.

Self-Reinvention

Self-reinvention is crucial to a company's success and longevity. It involves regularly evaluating and adapting new strategies, products, and processes to stay ahead of industry trends and to meet customers' evolving needs. Organizations that fail to self-reinvent become obsolete and lose market share. General Motors represents a classic example of how self-reinvention preserves corporate integrity over turbulent times. GM was founded in the early 1900s and became the most dominant player in the US automotive industry over the years. During its first 50 years of operations, it had no competitors. But for the second half of the 20th century, GM gradually lost its market share from 50 percent to slightly above 20 percent. During the 2008 global financial recession, GM recorded a 45 percent sales drop and over $30 billion in losses. GM filed for bankruptcy in 2009.[285] The company's historic success seems to have clouded leadership judgment and masked their alertness to the magnitude of the threat posed by the Japanese and German automakers.[286]

GM benefited from a $13.4 billion bailout package with the condition that the corporation demonstrate financial viability within three months.[286] The executives were tasked to develop a sustainable plan, without which no further government funding would be forthcoming. The executives resolved to split the company into two and migrated assets to a new company that would be fully funded by equity. The old company would inherit GM's liabilities. This proposal was received favorably, and GM benefited from a $50 billion equity injection.[287]

GM had three CEOs in rapid succession, but its turnaround was primarily credited to Mary Bara, who received unlimited company leadership support. By 2011, the company regained its title as the largest automobile producer globally.[287] The years following saw the company record billions in profits, and GM launched several eco-friendly car models.[288] GM's turnaround was credited to its leadership courage and ability to make tough choices without hesitation [286] At the center of GM's turnaround success was issue management—resolving issues long before they become problems through open communication and collaborative leadership. The leaders possessed the hallmarks of transformational leaders: always stimulating, questioning, and challenging the status quo. They had a strong vision for the future. Their strategic foresight led to their conviction that the future of GM is electric cars, and they must follow that path to continue to be profitable. The C-suite executives knew nothing lasted forever and were keenly monitoring the future.[286]

Innovative Growth

Innovative growth includes diversification, integration, and expansion. Integration is vertical growth, expansion is horizontal growth, and diversification combines both. An example of a successfully diversified corporate is Tata Motors of India. Tata expanded its market to 170 countries and pioneered developing products such as electric vehicles, trucks, buses, and defense vehicles. They were also continually investing in R&D and exploring cutting-edge technologies.[289]

Panoramic Integration

Businesses grow vertically by integrating backward and forward. Backward integration entails acquiring businesses that operate upstream, such as supply inputs or raw materials, while forward integration entails the acquisition of businesses that operate downstream in the supply chain, such as end-consumer products. The best example of backward and forward integration is in the oil industry, where companies integrate backward by expanding business on upstream activities such as exploration and drilling. They could also integrate forward by acquiring business in distribution and retail activities, derivatives, etc. In 2018, Abu Dhabi National Oil Company (ADNOC) announced it would invest $45 billion over five years to expand its downstream operations, including refining, petrochemicals, and gas processing.[290] This was a forward integration strategy for ADNOC, aiming to capture more value from its oil reserves by processing and selling higher-value products. ADNOC has also pursued acquiring or partnering with companies that supply inputs for its operations. For example, in 2019, ADNOC acquired a 70 percent stake in the chemical business of Borealis, which supplies ADNOC with polyolefin feedstock for its petrochemical operations.[290]

Prudent Expansion

Expansion entails vertical (scope) and horizontal (scale) growth. Expansion can be achieved in several ways, including mergers and acquisitions, opening new branches, investing in innovative technologies or product lines, and entering new markets or industries. Successful expansion can lead to increased revenue, market share, and profitability. However, expansion also carries risks, such as increased competition, higher costs, and organizational complexity.

Examples of successfully expanded corporations worldwide include Amazon, Toyota, Samsung, Unilever, Alibaba, and Reliance. Amazon expanded into a global e-commerce giant by acquiring Zappos and Whole Foods, expanding into India and Southeast Asia, and making a massive investment in e-commerce platforms.[291] Toyota opened manufacturing plants in the US, China, and India to increase its production capacity, better serve local markets, and invest in new technologies.[292] Samsung expanded into semiconductors, smartphones, and home appliances and invested heavily in new frontiers of technology, such as fifth-generation networks and foldable smartphones.[293] Unilever acquired Dove, Lipton, and Ben & Jerry's and entered a joint venture with Indian conglomerate Hindustan Unilever Limited.[100] Alibaba expanded into business-to-consumer, consumer-to-consumer, and cloud computing services and increased its global footprint.[294] Reliance Industries started as a textile manufacturer in 1966 and expanded into petrochemicals, refining, retail, and telecommunications.

Self-Cascading Reflections

The failure story of the Titanic and the turnaround success stories of Apple Corporation and General Motors provide multiple reflection questions. Let us now reflect on the following questions:

- Overall, what is our takeaway lesson from the tragic story of the Titanic from an organizational resilience point of view?
- What safeguards must we put in place to prevent overconfidence during periods of stability and success?
- How can we build resilience into our operations and supply chain to mitigate the impact of the crisis?
- How can we collaborate with other organizations or stakeholders to address the crisis and achieve shared goals?

- How can we measure progress and success during the crisis, and what metrics should we use to evaluate our performance?

Bend Your Mind!

Could the Titanic have been saved? Did it sink even before it set sail due to ship owners not hiring the right crew? The current global practice of hiring for senior corporate positions contains loopholes that often do not filter out toxic persons at the right time. Interviews and resumés are not enough. Attitudes, toxicity, and malicious hearts can never be examined from a resumé. Background checks may need to be enhanced for those assuming very senior positions. Once a person passes all the interviews and background checks, there may be a need to offer a period of open public feedback prior to confirmation, particularly for the most senior leadership positions, such as CEOs. Extended probation periods could also be applied in some cases. Leaders developed within the organizational hierarchy are more likely to grasp the operational culture and self-conduct ethically. Hence, policies geared toward growing and retaining home-grown talents are recommended.

Chapter Eight
SME RESILIENCE

Caterpillars morph into butterflies to see the fairer version of themselves. As they fly to explore new horizons and embrace new opportunities, they do not forget how they transformed through repeated ecdysis processes.

Springboard

Hello, Honey Badger!

When Mark Twain said, "It's not the size of the dog in the fight, it's the size of the fight in the dog," he probably would have picked "Honey Badger" for the nastiest animal and the hardest to beat in the animal kingdom. Weighing 31 pounds (14 kilograms) and measuring three feet long, the honey badger leaves any animal that lives to tell the story of their fight with expletives, including descriptions like ferocious, mean, ruthless, and savage.[295] The disproportionately extreme mammal has earned its honor as the most fearless animal on Earth. It converts a python into sausage. It takes on six lions and beats them senselessly.

Hyenas are no match for it, and even crocodiles must tread carefully because of their bad temper. Few predators dare to challenge it; it never backs down when attacked. If it does, it often only leaves the "boxing ring" not because of fear or fatigue but due to boredom.

Honey badgers have an incredible resilience quotient, able to survive in different habitat conditions from very dry aridity to very wet, and even reportedly able to swim and effectively hunt sea creatures underwater.[295] What makes these little creatures play in the same league as known rulers of the jungle and even survive in extreme conditions? The secrets of this remarkable mammal are just a few advantages that overcompensate for its smaller size: loose and very thick skin around the neck, strong jaws, an immunity to venom, a reversible anal pouch with a paralyzing stench, a voracious appetite, and a fearless attitude. The loose skin allows it to twist, turn, and bite back when attacked. The skin is so thick it can withstand an arrow shot, a spear, or the blow of a sharp machete. The teeth of predators leave honey badgers with very little material damage on the skin.[295]

In many ways, honey badgers' resilience symbolizes some small enterprises' resilience to perilous operating conditions. Like the lion or elephant seemingly outmatch the honey badger, resilient SMEs do not enjoy the many advantages of considerable size, yet they still survive hostile environments despite their resource constraints. This chapter examines the informal nature of SMEs and the various characteristics small enterprises can use to overcome adversity. The chapter draws insights from practical examples to discuss how small enterprises can move from a non-resilience state to a resilience state and sustain their resilience.

AN OVERVIEW OF SMES

World Bank estimates that 90 percent of all businesses across the globe are SMEs, and they account for over half of the world's employment.[296] These numbers vary from one region to the next. For instance, in the Organization for Economic Cooperation and Development countries (OECD), nearly 99 percent of business enterprises are SMEs, and at least 70 percent of employment is in the SME sector.[297] The numbers are comparatively lower in other regions, where SMEs account for 65 percent of jobs and contribute about 55 percent to the Gross Domestic Product.[298] However, the SME sector is vulnerable to disruptive shocks, calling for special attention to SME resilience metrics.[299]

The term SME is an acronym for Small and Medium-sized Enterprise. However, a universal definition of SME does not exist, as each country has different criteria for classifying an enterprise as an SME. A sampling of evidence points to over 50 definitions in 75 countries with heterogeneous terminologies, considerable inconsistencies, and perplexing ambiguities.[300] There seems to be a rainbow of definitions depending on the institution, national law, or industry. The most common criterion adopted across the world is employee headcount.[297] However, the growth of hybrid employment and the proliferation of tech-savvy industries increasingly challenge this criterion's reliability. To overcome this problem, some jurisdictions use more descriptors in addition to the number of employees, such as annual turnover and total assets. These definitional adjuncts, however, are where the confusion and disparity begin. For instance, according to the European Commission, a small enterprise has an annual turnover of $10.6 million and below. In Kenya, an enterprise with the same yearly turnover would pass under national law as a large corporation.[301] Similarly, what the World Bank classifies as a micro-enterprise would be, at minimum, referred to in Kenya as a medium-sized enterprise.[300]

This book prefers the qualitative definition of SMEs, as most SMEs share the same qualitative characteristics irrespective of employee headcount or financial metric differences. All SMEs are distinguishable by their simple structures and rudimentary business practices. Decision-making in SMEs is often the sole prerogative of the manager, who doubles up as the owner and the technical person in direct contact with customers, suppliers, bankers, and the authorities. In contrast to large corporations, SMEs enjoy much decision-making autonomy and freedom of control.

SMEs are an integral part of the global economy, and their resilience is key to fostering economic growth and job creation. Not only do they provide a substantial proportion of employment, but they also contribute to the innovation and dynamism which keeps economies competitive. SMEs positively impact household living standards, often providing more affordable goods and services than larger businesses. As such, the resilience of SMEs is critical for improving living standards.

The SME sector is distinct from other business sectors in size, resources, and challenges. SMEs are typically small and often lack resources compared to larger corporates. This makes them more vulnerable to external shocks, such as economic downturns or regulation changes. SMEs also tend to have smaller networks, making it difficult to access resources or capital. SMEs face unique challenges, and staying resilient is key to their success. Resilience helps SMEs deal with difficult and unpredictable conditions under which they often operate, enabling them to survive and thrive in a constantly changing landscape. The typical SME commands a very insignificant market share, is often owner-funded, and rarely possesses a financial buffer. Most SMEs face resource-constraint challenges that expose them to higher vulnerabilities than large corporations. They operate on a highly lean human capital base, are frequently underfunded, and lack managerial expertise, the necessary technology, and the institutional capacity to compete effectively in the marketplace.[302] These qualitative characteristics are central to understanding and setting up SMEs for resilience.

SME RESILIENCE DRIVERS

Fadzil & Rashid propose an SME resilience framework that comprises ten pillars: review and adjust business operations to suit current needs, transition into new areas of business, apply better management practices, develop human resources, resize the scale of business to bring down costs, solicit for government grants and financial assistance, go digital, optimize capital savings, ramp up marketing efficiency, and diversify products.[303] These propositions provide the much-needed mental model for SME resilience. They are, therefore, a good starting point for policymaking. However, this framework lacks practical illustrations to demonstrate how the inherent policy options are applied in real life. Earlier in 2015, Seville, Van Opstal, & Vargo presented the following set of principles for SME resilience:

making adaptive capacity a core competency, becoming a learning organization, building social capital, designing resilience into operational excellence, looking beyond risk to see opportunities, and embarking on the "rough road" to stability.[304] This section of the book builds on the works of Seville, Van Opstal, & Vargo to present a mental model for SME resilience. SMEs have advantages that give them a good head start in the resilience development journey, such as being less procedural and having short decision chains, flexibility, fast adaptability, and fast learning.[305] Based on the Seville, Van Opstal, & Vargo model, this section discusses some core resilience drivers: adaptive capacity, learning, social capital, risk reframing, resilience journey, and operational excellence.

Adaptive Capacity

Adaptive resilience is a function of adaptive capacity. It includes the knowledge, material resource endowments, and demeanor that can facilitate timely structural changes in doing business in response to environmental disruption. Before the COVID-19 pandemic, the higher education sector in Kenya had already experienced significant disruption triggered by macro-changes in the regulatory environment, leading to a substantial drop in the number of students who attain university entry grades. For a long time, universities thrived on high demand for higher education, but at that time, they suddenly found themselves operating below capacity. Many universities consequently shut down their satellite campuses, and some private universities were either ordered by the regulator to close due to fiscal insolvency or given a two-year grace period to settle their debts or face closure.[306]

Adaptive capacity was the critical factor that enabled PAC University to lead resilience to the COVID-19 pandemic in Kenya's higher education sector.[307] The university has a history that dates to the 1970s. For a long time, the university conducted physical classes on its two campuses in Nairobi City. However, over this period, the university also offered most of its postgraduate programs online, punctuated with a few face-to-face classes. To adapt to changing market conditions, PAC University started transitioning most of its courses from face-to-face to online learning, as doing so provided the advantage of collapsing several physical classes into one, significantly reducing operational costs. The market turmoil in Kenya's education sector was severely aggravated by the COVID-19 pandemic, which triggered a national lockdown. However, instead of disrupting its operations, the university took full advantage of the shutdown to accelerate online learning.

PAC University demonstrated adaptive capacity as a core attribute of its resilience leadership strategy. The university long recognized that the future sustainability of universities lies in building capacity for online teaching and learning. Hence, it became very intentional in its digital transformation agenda, which paid off—PAC University was well ahead of its peers when it became apparent that the pandemic was not relenting any time soon, and there was a need for learning to sustain through online modes. This earned the university a name in the East African region as a center of excellence for online teaching and learning. In 2021, the university won a highly competitive tender from the German Development Corporation, which saw it train 240 staff from 30 universities in six countries of East Africa on digital skills for online teaching and learning.[308]

Learning

What is apparent throughout the resilience story of PAC University is that it became a learning organization. The leadership demonstrated an openness to new ideas, encouraging knowledge sharing, which transformed every participant in the change process into an agent of knowledge cross-pollination.[309] This was particularly exemplified at the onset of the transformation journey. To increase capacity, the university quickly developed a critical mass of its teaching staff as online learning champions subjected to an intense training-of-trainers program. Their adaptive transformation for the pandemic reflected the traits that set learning organizations apart. These are the creation, acquisition, interpretation, transference, and retention of knowledge and the intentional modification of behavior considering new knowledge and insights. The online learning champions underwent a rigorous process of learning how to develop syllabuses for online learning, the various technology tools available for online teaching and learning, and the user skills for effective delivery of teaching. The online learning champions were then deployed to teach others online pedagogy skills and orient them on a relearning management system that brought classroom experience into the online space. These also helped create customizable templates and user manuals that transformed knowledge from tacit into explicit, enabling scalable knowledge transfer.

They were utilized to conduct regular training, especially targeting new students and staff.

Frequent refresher training was also conducted to update user skills as new possibilities emerged. These included integrating the learning management system with other collaborative technologies (such as Zoom) and deploying a lockdown browser when administering exams online. During the various sessions, conversations were encouraged around systems thinking, creativity, and continuous discovery, with lecturers given to experiment with various ways of leveraging social media to enrich the online learning experience. A feedback loop system was created, drawing attention to what was being done well and where there was room for improvement at the individual and team levels. Among these was the need to abandon the old-fashioned lecture room, mental model and adopt a new identity as a facilitator and knowledge co-creator. Today, the university prides itself on a thriving community of creativity and innovation.[307]

Social Capital

Undercover Billionaire, presented by Glenn Stearns on the Discovery Channel, is a perfect example of how to build social capital from scratch. The show camouflages itself as a documentary about self-made billionaires building an enterprise from scratch. They must do so within three months in a foreign land full of strangers, with only a fueled old truck, a hundred dollars in their wallet, a phone, and zero contacts. Thus, it symbolizes the typical situation most SMEs find themselves in, such as resource constraints, insignificant (if not zero) brand identity, and the thin line between the business and its owner. Whereas the SMEs were built from scratch, most episodes were conducted during the COVID-19 pandemic, providing a perfect context for learning about SME resilience and how to build and leverage social capital to overcome difficult conditions. Cataclysmic events such as the COVID-19 pandemic often disrupt SMEs to the point of starting all over again from scratch, just like *Undercover Billionaire* showcased.

Social capital is simply the resources or goodwill that subsists in relationships.[310] It includes the sum of actual and potential resources available through and derived from and mobilized in an individual's network of relationships. [311] The rationale behind social capital and its contribution to SME resilience is that interpersonal relationships matter. [312] Social networks have value as social contacts affect the sustainability of individuals and enterprises.[313] The significance of social capital for SME resilience is that social capital provides useful support when needed. Social capital confers information, influence, control, and social solidarity. An individual's social capital is the contacts they hold and how their contacts link them to other patterns of relations.[314]

Social capital is typically built through networking, which is simply about establishing and maintaining lines of communication with people. The focus of networking is building relationships. This is done through feelings of gratitude, reciprocity, respect, and friendships, which are sources of information and opportunities and, in certain circumstances, may be used as a form of reputation. Creating a social network is a process, not an event. It calls for patience, as you cannot have an instant rapport with everyone.

Building social capital takes courage, creativity, and commitment. As Glean Stearns puts it, "You must meet people. You cannot get anywhere without people."[311] Social capital is built by getting to know people, finding out how to help them, and taking notes on what they can do for you. In any community, there are always people who are willing to help. However, it takes humility, resourcefulness, making oneself useful, and an attitude of gratitude. Social capital is also built by reciprocating kindness, building mutual trust, and finding ways of collaborating so that together, everyone achieves more. Within any community, there is always someone who knows someone who carries the key to a breakthrough for your business. That someone can be just about anyone. It may be the city's governor, the local community hospital gatekeeper, or even that beggar across the street.

Risk Reframing

One of the realities confronting SMEs during adversity is operating in survival mode, which sets the enterprise on an endless daily grind of struggling to keep operations going. If the lessons from *Undercover Billionaire* are anything to go by, operating in survival mode denies the business owner the time to think and plan more strategically about how to grow from one level of resilience to another. Operating in survival mode clouds the business owner's judgment about what is important, making it difficult to look beyond risks to see potential opportunities. Seeing the opportunity *in* the risk calls for positive thinking, focus, thinking ahead, and visualizing the future. The positive thinker sees the invisible, feels the intangible, and achieves the impossible. [315] They activate not their fears but their hopes and dreams, focusing on the possibilities ahead. When they fail, they look for alternative solutions because they believe there is always an opportunity.

For SMEs, countless opportunities abound in challenging times. Looking beyond the risks to see opportunity begins with the belief that there is always a way to benefit from what, at face value, appears to be adversity. During the COVID-19 pandemic, many SMEs pivoted to making masks, and even hand sanitizers as demand for those products outstripped supply. One such SME is Shine Distillery & Grill, a restaurant in the US that started producing and selling private-label hand sanitizers. According to media reports, business picked up quickly, and, for its owners, this kind of pivoting became a game-changer—especially as the restaurant business ground to a halt due to the lockdown. [316]

Opportunities also exist in local resources, so it is important to tap into them. Small business development centers, incubators, and financiers are among those that are open. Small business development centers are designed to build upon the entrepreneur's disciplinary knowledge and assist them in learning the basic skills to build a business, from the initial bright idea to a fully developed concept that maps and validates the path of the idea to its scale up. [317] Since small business development centers are usually networked with many like-minded enterprises and organizations in the community (locally and beyond), successful incubation signals a stamp of approval that can give SMEs an edge when raising additional capital or getting linkages with such networks. [318] While usually designed for startups, opportunities in small business development centers and incubators are accessible to virtually any SME and can be a perfect avenue for business reinvention.

Resilience Journey

Resilience is not a goal nor a means to a goal. Resilience is a way of life. This simple fact applies to organizations just as it does to individuals. It is better to think of resilience as "an emergent property of a complex system, meaning that it is difficult to design a truly resilient system—it must evolve naturally from interactions between its constituent parts."[319] Thus, it is more befitting to think of it as the road *of* resilience rather than the road *to* resilience. Resilience thinking is the innate or acquired mindset that believes that disruptive events will happen eventually. Therefore, some semblance of preparedness is needed to manage them even when their cause, nature, probability, and impact cannot be estimated ahead of time. This call is not exclusive to large corporations, as the same principles can be applied to the SME sector. Military-style discipline is needed to propel SMEs toward the road of resilience.

SMEs need to pursue business resilience as a strategic initiative based on the conviction that it is upon resilience that sustainable competitive advantage is more likely. This is an intentional process of resource accumulation and development intended to build capacity to attain a specified operational or strategic objective—namely, to create resilience capacity. Whereas resource constraints present a crucial dilemma for SMEs seeking to build resilience, various options remain open. One example is a reputational reserve, which only needs the SME to be authentic, ethical, and of high integrity. Integrity generates external legitimacy within the business community, which can be the sole lifeline for SMEs in times of distress. In contrast, a dubious and dodgy character erodes trust, the currency of exchange in business relationships, just like in any other relationship.

While market dynamics differ from country to country during recessions and other economic shocks, the fundamentals of risks and opportunities are essentially the same across the board. However, a lot relies on the business owner as the enterprise leader in navigating the rough road of resilience. Resilience-oriented SME leaders are keen to pursue organic growth, fully aware that fast growth is, for SMEs, one of the deadliest enemies of sustainability. They have the execution intelligence to embed resilience into operational excellence, with enough foresight to decipher the underlying opportunities that can ratchet up their resilience posture. They also have the hindsight to set appropriate limits on the risks and opportunities the enterprise can take.

Operational Excellence

Operational excellence refers to continuous improvement to optimize capacity and efficiently deploy resources to maximize value creation.[320] However, increased disruptions of business operations due to disruptive shocks are causing managers to question the wisdom that birthed the lean operations philosophy. This questioning saw the emergence of the "leagile" paradigm as the delicate balancing of *lean* management with *agility* to overcome the no-longer-tenable assumption of lean management that demand will always be predictable.[321]

Today, business discourse gradually gravitates toward embedding resilience into operations as a new paradigm in operations management thinking due to the failure of leagile management practices to offer foolproof solutions to operational challenges during disruptive shocks. Small enterprises are inherently leagile. Due to resource constraints, SMEs are typically lean in their operations. Secondly, SMEs are more agile since there are no bureaucratic layers of the decision-making process that typically characterize large corporations. These two resilience properties make SMEs more flexible and readily adaptive to operational disruptions, making up for their resource constraints. Given their leagility, operational resilience excellence is conceived of as regular incremental improvements to the resilience of SME business operations with the twin objective of surviving unanticipated operational shocks while optimizing scarce resources.

Small business enterprises can embed resilience into operational excellence "by preparing actively for adversity, developing contingency plans, building networks and critically examining their adaptive behaviors."[322] For SMEs, active preparation for turbulence primarily entails building a financial buffer through organic growth or keeping debt loads as light as possible if the debt is at all unavoidable. A reputational buffer also does not require any capital commitment and thus provides a viable option. Besides buffer building, SMEs can develop anticipatory capabilities to sense critical developments in their operating environment and activate a timely response plan. Lessons from past disruptions that either affected the enterprise or were drawn from the experiences of other SMEs provide learning opportunities for setting contingency plans in case of a similar incident.

Small enterprises should also periodically appraise their resilience posture by enrolling professional help. Many SMEs lack a sounding board to appraise their operational resilience excellence and give feedback for improvement. The wise SME allows for periodic independent operations assessment for enterprise resilience. *Undercover Billionaire* demonstrates that successful entrepreneurs frequently seek feedback from industry professionals attached to the local small business development agencies, providing an independent perspective of where the SME stands in the enterprise resilience-vulnerability matrix.

Self-Cascading Reflections

SMEs often face limited financial resources, and staying resilient is even more challenging. One example of a small enterprise that survived a crisis is the Scottish brewery BrewDog. During the global financial crisis of 2008, the company struggled to secure funding to expand its business. BrewDog focused on its unique craft beer offerings, which were gaining popularity among consumers. The company launched an online shop and managed to reach a broader clientele. It also built customer relationships through social media, feedback, and interactions. The company launched a crowdfunding campaign and successfully raised over a million pounds. As we consider the business model of BrewDog, let us now reflect on the following questions:

- What core competencies does our organization have, and how can we focus on them to deliver better products or services to our customers?
- How can we leverage technology to streamline our processes, reach a wider audience, and reduce costs?
- What external funding options are available, and how can we secure funding to grow our business?
- How can we prioritize customer service to build a loyal customer base that will recommend our business to others?
- What financial metrics should we monitor closely, and how can we reduce unnecessary expenses while investing in areas that will help our business grow?
- How can we stay flexible and adaptable to market and industry trends, and what steps can we take to pivot our business model or adjust our product or service offerings?

Bend Your Mind!

The metamorphosis of a butterfly is a multi-stage process of change and growth. An egg laid by a female butterfly on a plant leaf hatches into a tiny caterpillar that passes through several stages of development, shedding skin repeatedly in a process known as ecdysis until it morphs into a fully grown pupa or chrysalis. From there, it transforms into a beautiful butterfly. It emerges from the chrysalis and spreads its wings, ready to fly, explore the world, and entertain our eyes.

The transformation story of a butterfly is often used as a metaphor for personal growth and change, as it represents the idea of overcoming challenges and emerging a stronger and more beautiful version of oneself. The metamorphosis story of the butterfly is a metaphor for the growth and resilience of SMEs. SMEs embrace change, as their growth and transformation require leaving behind what used to be comfortable and familiar. SMEs require an unclouded vision and resilience posture to take proactive steps toward the future they aspire to realize. SMEs leverage adversity and endure pain to grow and transform. SMEs' growth into sustainable businesses requires investment, sacrifices, and perseverance. Butterflies see new horizons and embrace opportunities that caterpillars never had. But to exploit them, SMEs require bold skin and resilient leadership.

Chapter Nine
NONPROFIT SECTOR RESILIENCE

Value perception is as exclusive as DNA, as inimitable as a fingerprint, and as peculiar as feeling. See the bodily motion of a baby breastfed by a loving mom. See the face of the mother.

Springboard

t is well with my soul. Horatio Gates Spafford, you are here, eternally here!

"The water is three miles deep." A captain's voice floated above a philanthropist.[323] In the captain's hand was a voyage map. They were sailing right over where a disaster happened, a shipwreck in the Atlantic Ocean that would forever change the life of Horatio Gates Spafford and that of 226 other families. His four daughters were among those who perished, and his wife was plucked unconscious from a plank of floating wood.[323] Earlier in his life, the philanthropist had survived a devastating fire that killed 300 people and left over 100,000 city residents homeless.

His home had become a refuge for the fire victims, where they embraced, fed, cared for the injured, and helped those in need. The ship's wreckage, known as the Ville Du Havre, happened in 1873. However, the story of the character of the philanthropist and his charitable community that defied all the odds became a media sensation that earned them the name "Overcomers."[323]

More than 150 years later, many churches worldwide sing, "It Is Well with My Soul," a hymn the philanthropist wrote after receiving the sobering news about the wreckage from the captain. Not only that, but the story of the philanthropist continues to be the inspiration behind countless pieces of literature, one of which became so impactful that it won the author the Nobel Peace Prize.[324] Today, the legacy of the charitable community Horatio founded still lives on in the name of a renowned children's hospital in Jerusalem City.

The preceding is the legendary story of Horatio Gates Spafford, an epitome of resilience and one of the early fathers of the nonprofit world. The story demonstrates that nonprofit formations are not spared from the predicaments arising from environmental jolts. However, like any other resilient enterprise, nonprofits can also build resiliency into their systems to overcome adversity and continue their journey, despite existential realities.

This chapter examines the nonprofit sector's nature and key resilience drivers. The chapter focuses on seven distinct nonprofit organizations, from which it offers a synthesis of the basic principles that actors in the nonprofit sector can apply to make their organizations more resilient to disruptive events. A brief overview of the operating landscape is presented for each nonprofit formation, and the unique dynamics of the subsector are highlighted.

NONPROFIT WORLD OVERVIEW

The history of nonprofit organizations dates back to the 1800s, although some organizations that fit the nonprofit category have existed since ancient times.[325] Nonprofit organizations are non-state formations that exist to create value without a profit motive. When activities are undertaken to generate profit, the proceeds are utilized for purposes other than to generate wealth for its owners. Sometimes, "nonprofit" is used interchangeably with "non-governmental organizations" (NGOs), as NGOs constitute most, if not all, of the nonprofit sector in many jurisdictions. NGOs are private organizations that pursue activities to relieve suffering, promote the interests of people experiencing poverty, protect the environment, provide essential social services, or undertake community development.[326] The common factor in all NGOs is that "they have a mission for which they mobilize support, influence governments, raise funds, educate the public, dedicate resources or represent its members."[326] For this book, nonprofit organizations will be used interchangeably with NGOs as an umbrella term that refers to charitable, community organizations, civil society, or social enterprises, so long as they have a social mission as their primary or sole reason for existence.

The NGO sector is characterized by extreme diversity, heterogeneity, and a broad spectrum of goals, structures, and motivations.[327] Some NGOs are well-resourced and affluent, boasting millions or billions in annual budgets. Others lead a fragile hand-to-mouth existence, struggling to survive from one year to the next. Large and established NGOs have a highly professional staff, while others rely heavily on volunteers and supporters—some of whose technical competencies do not always align with program requirements.[326] Resource constraints are a characteristic feature of many NGOs, inhibiting them from undertaking long-term initiatives. Some NGOs operate where government aid is not possible or government services are not accessible. The very existence of NGOs is largely due to the limitations of the government as the agent of the distribution of public goods.[328] In terms of numbers, it is estimated that there are at least ten million NGOs worldwide. However, the number of nonprofit organizations is much higher since not all nonprofit organizations are registered with the authority regulating NGOs.

The resilience of nonprofit organizations is critical because of their role as the backbone of resilience in society, especially during calamities. They are usually the first responders in cataclysms and are sometimes even resorted to by the business community as the last defense against distress. They are to society what soldiers are to a country. They are resilience support agents in many ways. They provide essential services such as food relief and medical care to disaster victims, build community resilience through resources and skills, and advocate for the vulnerable in their societies. They work with the public and private sectors to build more resilient systems. While NGOs are just as susceptible to adversity as any other organizations, they are some of the most resilient. Some NGOs operate on short-term grants, often one-off transactional arrangements earmarked to achieve a specific purpose. As such, sponsors lack the incentive to care about the NGO's actual cost and often impose grant restrictions. Unlike the for-profit sector, which only faces a fall in service demand in times of depression or other disruptive disasters, NGOs face the twin problem of resource constraints and high demand for their services. In the wake of the COVID-19 pandemic, a study that sampled 388 NGOs found that "63% saw their funding decrease during the pandemic, and for many, this decrease in grants coincided with a sharp increase in demand for services."[329]

The nonprofit sector has seen its fair share of struggles and triumphs. It has been at the forefront of many of the greatest achievements and faced tremendous adversity. But despite the odds, nonprofit organizations have demonstrated remarkable resilience. They have persevered through financial hardship, regulatory upheaval, and political uncertainty. They have adapted to changing markets and shifting consumer preferences. They have embraced modern technologies and innovative strategies. They have shown inspiring tenacity and fortitude in adversity. They have demonstrated unmatched courage, perseverance, and strength in volatile situations.

This chapter discusses nonprofit sector resilience to systemic disruption. Due to their diversity in form, structure, focus, and operational context, each subsector is examined to aggregate a set of resilience principles. For this purpose, the nonprofit sector is divided into seven generic organizational archetypes: faith-based organizations, humanitarian organizations, labor unions, professional associations, development organizations, social enterprises, and community-based organizations.

FAITH-BASED ORGANIZATIONS

Faith-based organizations (FBOs), while varying in form, invoke images of places of gathering in worship. FBOs either have an affiliation to or were founded by a religious organization. Like all other institutions with a social mission, religious organizations play a critical role in resilience building—not just because of their solid grassroots presence but, perhaps even more importantly, the psychological property of faith in adaptability. They create a sense of meaning in adversity and hope for a better tomorrow, generating positive energy and creativity.[330]

So significant is religion in times of great calamities that even governments resort to religious organizations as channels of divine intervention and restoration. It is not uncommon for governments worldwide to call for a National Day of Prayer and Fasting in crises and emergencies. For instance, President George Bush declared a National Prayer Day after the 9/11 terror attack.[331] Perhaps no other calamity more deservedly led to the proclamation of a Day of National Prayer worldwide like the COVID-19 pandemic, signifying the resilience function of faith. During the COVID-19 pandemic, many churches, mosques, and synagogues became places of respite, offering support and assistance by turning their facilities into venues for various purposes, such as food banks and distribution centers for essential supplies.

Like other nonprofit organizations, religious organizations rely on various revenue sources to fund their operations and programs. These can include tithes and offerings from members and attendees, grants and other forms of philanthropic support, and income from fundraising events and activities. Some generate revenue from renting or leasing their facilities or selling products such as books, music, or other materials related to their mission and activities. However, tithes and offerings are the primary funding source for most religious organizations. When the COVID-19 pandemic triggered a national lockdown and prohibition of social gatherings, religious organizations were among the hardest hit due to precautionary measures such as social distancing and a ban on social gatherings.

Like any other organization, many religious organizations must devise novel ways to cope with disruption quickly. This was most manifest in the wake of the COVID-19 pandemic. One such religious organization is the Calvary Presbyterian Church in North Dakota, US. It began holding drive-in services in its parking lot, with sound amplified using a PA system mounted atop a flat truck and broadcast through a short-range frequency mode transmitter to congregants via their vehicles' radios. They did this throughout the pandemic and even created an outdoor worship stage to increase the prospects of hosting events. "We never missed a Sunday," the pastor quipped.[332]

HUMANITARIAN ORGANIZATIONS

Humanitarian organizations are a class of NGOs whose mission is to respond to victims of crises such as natural disasters, wars, and other emergencies. Despite being a multi-billion-dollar subsector, the structure of the humanitarian landscape is a risk factor for resilience building for many humanitarian organizations. Among the challenges

NGOs face are corrosive competition, resource imbalance, and many intermediaries in the humanitarian value chain. Less than 1 percent of all humanitarian funding goes to local NGOs. Further, the short-term nature of contracts makes the operating environment very unpredictable and causes high financial uncertainty.[327]

Some resilient humanitarian agencies have developed sustainable ways of navigating donor-funding-related financial uncertainty to keep their operations going. One example is Partners in Health, an international NGO with a presence in underprivileged and remote communities located in 12 countries. This NGO operates multiple income-generating social enterprises, such as pharmacies and food processing. For instance, in Haiti, the NGO runs a comprehensive peanut production program that involves harvesting peanuts from a 30-acre farm that employs local farmers or purchasing them from a cooperative of 200 smallholders. The proceeds from these enterprises are used to support the NGO's humanitarian assistance programs. When the COVID-19 pandemic hit, the NGO set up various COVID-19 treatment centers, besides providing food, water, and other health relief supplies.[333]

Their operation in emergencies makes organizations in the humanitarian sector among the most resilient in the world. Many humanitarian organizations have emergency response plans and perform regular drills to assess and enhance their readiness for disruption or crisis. One such organization is the Red Cross, a humanitarian agency with an illustrious history that dates to the 1800s. The Red Cross is resilient due to its robust systems and processes for disaster response, including training volunteers, stockpiling supplies, and forming partnerships with like-minded organizations. Consequently, the organization gets support from an extensive network of donors and volunteers, providing adequate human and material resources to sustain operations regardless of the magnitude or frequency of disruption. Over the years, the Red Cross has built a strong brand, which has earned it a reputational capital that comes in handy during times of crisis.

LABOR UNIONS

Labor Unions, also referred to as trade unions, are nonprofit organizations whose mission is to represent the collective interests of employees in a particular sector. Accordingly, they are member-based organizations that draw their membership from people who work in the same profession or field of occupation. Their operations are sustained by levying membership dues, the amount of which is dependent on the wages and salaries earned by its members. In addition, labor unions also undertake investments that generate income and conduct fundraising to support their activities. A core business of labor unions is to advocate for employees' rights and protect their jobs' security. Because disruptive shocks often trigger massive job losses, labor unions are among the nonprofit organizations that are most impacted by disruptive shocks.

Many labor unions worldwide have grappled with falling membership in the last few decades. Trade union decline has been reported worldwide, especially in relatively more advanced economies, including the US, Asia, and Europe. [334] One dominant factor cited for the growing extinction of labor unions is the age of automation and the rise of temporary employment. Hitherto representing a large share of the workforce and covering many employees under collective bargaining agreements, labor unions have become increasingly threatened by the emergence of a jobless economy propelled by advances in artificial intelligence and the digital revolution.[335]

As the COVID-19 pandemic has exemplified, the cataclysm of the 21st century has only deepened the existential predicaments of labor unions. With many unionized workers experiencing layoffs, resilient unions adapted by negotiating terms of employment such as reduced hours and temporary wage cuts as an alternative to outright retrenchment. Unions have also advocated for implementing paid leave policies to support members affected by the pandemic. For instance, a union in the United States known as Service Employees International Union played a critical part in the negotiations that resulted in the passage of the Families First Coronavirus Response Act (FFCRA). FFCRA provided emergency paid sick leave and expanded family and medical leave for workers affected by the pandemic. While instrumental in protecting labor unions at their base, these measures only explain the temporary relevance of unions. Surviving the realities of a jobless economy calls for a paradigm shift in union thinking toward a redefinition of whom unions represent, what goals they should pursue, and which strategies they should embrace. They have an opportunity to reinvent themselves as unions of self-employed workers and advocates of the rights of digital workers.

PROFESSIONAL ASSOCIATIONS

Professional associations exist to promote high professional standards, provide an opportunity for continuous professional development, and advocate for the profession's and its members' rights. Like labor unions, the operations of professional associations are funded by their members through membership levies. The sustenance of the professional association depends on the ability of its members to continue generating income either as employees or private practitioners.

The adaptability of professional associations calls for implementing a range of measures. Some professional associations resort to austerity measures, such as cutting non-essential expenses and staff retrenchment. However, more resilient professional associations become more innovative and introduce new services to boost their revenue streams. During the COVID-19 pandemic, professional associations shifted to virtual formats for meetings and events and sought alternative means of revenue generation. Others introduced online courses that appealed to both members and non-members. Professional associations also undertook research consultancy services and developed resource materials for sale. These resources are typically related to the professional association's expertise, with some entailing advice or guidance on best practices. Industry partners and companies in the sector offer collaboration opportunities on projects such as research, professional development, and other activities related to the association's mission. An example is the International Council of Nurses, a professional association representing nurses globally. The association published numerous studies on how the COVID-19 pandemic affected nurses, including suggestions on how the threats to the profession can be mitigated.[336] Some of the association's publications were made available to the general public through a fee payable online.

DEVELOPMENT ORGANIZATIONS

The vital role of community development in resilience building makes the resilience of development organizations an essential topic for managers, leaders, and development practitioners. Development organizations work to improve the resilience conditions of communities in developing and marginalized communities. They build the proficiency of vulnerable communities experiencing natural- and human-made disasters to anticipate, prevent, recover from, and rebuild from shocks and stresses.[337] They improve access to essential services such as health and sanitation, support the development of strong and effective institutions, support small businesses and stimulate investment, provide training and resources, and foster social cohesion, which fosters a united response to adversity.

Both development and humanitarian organizations increase communities' abilities to cope with environmental shocks. However, while humanitarian organizations focus on providing relief to disaster victims, development organizations—by their very name—are intended to prevent vulnerability to future disasters by building community resilience. Thus, development organizations are proactive (preventive), and humanitarian organizations are reactive (curative). Hence, development organizations operate long-term, while humanitarian organizations address short-to medium-term emergencies.

Notwithstanding their uniqueness, development organizations differ from humanitarian organizations regarding their operating environment, apart from the fact that response to emergencies is not their primary concern. As such, humanitarian organizations' sustainability challenges (such as donor funding and demand sustenance) equally affect development organizations. Therefore, their existence and growth depend on how they navigate those challenges.

Microfinance institutions (MFIs) are among the development organizations severely disrupted by the COVID-19 pandemic due to the economic shocks on the vulnerable communities they serve. Many MFIs that were already struggling found themselves in a liquidity crisis.[338] However, resilient MFIs devised various strategies to adapt, such as leveraging technology, providing remote access to financial services, introducing new products (such as digital health insurance), and partnering with other development organizations and technology companies. Others extended moratoriums on loan repayment and became last-mile channels of distribution of COVID-19 grants. One example is Advans MFI, which offers financial services to underserved populations in several countries in Africa and Asia. Like many other organizations, Advans quickly adapted to remote working and had a team of HR staff regularly call their more than 600 staff to reassure them and listen to their needs. The MFI also negotiated the relaxation of financial covenants and activated resource buffers from its development partners.[338]

COMMUNITY-BASED ORGANIZATIONS

Community-Based Organizations (CBOs), sometimes called welfare societies, are local development-oriented organizations started by community members who organize together to undertake projects and programs to improve the quality of life. Unlike NGOs, which sometimes have a national or international footprint, CBOs are typically restricted to a small, specific neighborhood or local area. The founders and members are typically people from the community they operate in. The demographic composition of members is usually diverse and sometimes cross-cuts religions, professions, and political affiliations.[339] Members account for the most significant share of CBO activities' human and material resource provisions. However, like most nonprofit organizations, CBOs rely on volunteers and donations to undertake their activities—although many engage in self-sustaining income-generating activities. Like other development organizations, CBOs are vital players in the organizational resilience ecosystem. At the micro-level, they play a unique role in society by addressing local issues and needs, typically by actively empowering community members to participate in activities designed to improve their lives and neighborhoods.

During challenging times, CBOs provide essential services such as nutrition, shelter, healthcare, and education to underserved populations. They create a sense of community, an important ingredient for community resilience. Many CBOs are agents of economic development and useful resources for stimulating economic growth in their local area. They also serve as advocacy channels, giving voice to otherwise voiceless or disadvantaged members of society. They are an essential support system for many needy members of the local community. Therefore, they are important last-mile partners in the total development value chain and are frequently relied on by governments, national NGOs, international development organizations, and private foundations to achieve social objectives.

Due to their localized nature, many CBOs are small. Therefore, like SMEs, they also grapple with size challenges, among which are resource constraints. Resilient CBOs, however, find ways of adapting. When the COVID-19 pandemic disrupted operations, agile CBOs quickly shifted operations to virtual platforms, such as conducting meetings and trainings online. Others found ways to continue serving their communities by responding to the emerging needs occasioned by the disruption.

An example is North Brooklyn Mutual Aid Network (NBMAN), a grassroots CBO in a low-income community in New York. The CBO relies on volunteers for the workforce and boasts over 900 volunteers. When the COVID-19 pandemic hit, NBMAN experienced a spike in demand for its services on the one hand and a shortage of volunteers and supplies on the other. To continue serving the community, the NBMAN quickly set up systems for the contactless delivery of essential services, recruited new volunteers through social media, and established partnerships with other organizations to bridge resource deficits. The CBO readily adapted to demand, which shifted to diapers. They responded by opening a "diaper bank." They also pivoted from the food bank to cleanup brigades and partnered with a local community education council to facilitate remote learning by offering students tablets and other electronic devices.[(340)]

Another example is Mathare Environmental Conservation Youth Group (MECYG), a CBO based in one of the largest informal settlements in Nairobi City in Kenya. MECYG promotes environmental conservation and sustainable development in the local community through tree planting, waste management, and education programs. MECYG relied on donor funding for most of its activities. The COVID-19 pandemic occasioned a sudden decline in funding and resources. However, MECYG quickly adapted by shifting education programs to virtual platforms and began a home-composting program that saw community members reduce waste.[(341)]

In India, Aravind, a network of eye hospitals that began in the 1970s as a self-help group, adapted to the COVID-19 disruption by offering new products and services. Today, it is a chain of eye hospitals that provide free or heavily subsidized eye care services to poor people in remote villages in India.[(342)] When the pandemic hit, Aravind faced many challenges, including disruptions to its supply chain and decreased clientele. In response, Aravind started offering telemedicine services and launched an online store to sell eyeglasses and other products. It also developed a new business model to offer virtual training programs to other eye care providers.

PRIVATE FOUNDATIONS

A foundation is a nonprofit organization that primarily funds charitable causes or supports specific organizations or initiatives. An individual, a family, or a company can fund a foundation. Most large organizations and wealthy families start a private foundation as a distinct legal entity that accords them a formal structure to advance their charitable intentions.[343] The significance of private foundations for building resilient ecosystems cannot be gainsaid. According to a report by the OECD, private foundations in high-income countries committed at least one billion dollars—while the ones in developing countries committed around $600 million—in response to the COVID-19 pandemic by the end of 2022.

Foundations have one upside that distinguishes them from other nonprofit organizations: endowment, a fund invested in a diversified portfolio of assets to serve as a long-term source of finance for its cause. They also leverage significant non-financial assets such as relationships with influential persons.[343] On the downside, what is also unique about private foundations and which pose a serious resilience risk factor is that, unlike other forms of nonprofit organizations, they are prohibited by law from active solicitation of funds from the public or raising funds from external sources in the same way that public charities do, in as much as they are allowed to accept funds when offered. Further, reality suggests that not all foundations possess endowments. Instead, private foundations, most often than not, rely on allotments from the companies that started them.[344]

From the vantage point of private foundations, resilience is reflected in "the ability of grantees to achieve long-term aims amid significant disruptions in context collectively."[345] This means that the resilience of private foundations is not just a function of the sponsoring corporation's resilience, but also the grantee's resilience. This presents an additional challenge to the foundations' managers.

The Underdog Entrepreneur Foundation, a small foundation birthed in the post-COVID-19 era, devised creative ways to overcome this twin challenge. The foundation was started by a real estate mogul who seeded it with 50 thousand dollars to provide small business grants to qualifying applicants. The foundation awards grants as reimbursable expenses of up to five thousand dollars. This philanthropic strategy helps ensure that only serious applicants who have demonstrated a basic level of resilience that can be strengthened benefit from the fund. The nonprofit quickly metamorphosed by partnering with a local community foundation, which keeps it on track for sustainable growth.[346] This effectively opened up multiple fundraising pathways, which the foundation leveraged. Among these is the sale of merchandise such as branded T-shirts, spices, coffee, and toy products. The foundation also fundraises donations on its website, which provides a quick link to an online portal where people can donate through PayPal or credit card. Diversifying funding sources reduces the risk of relying on one income stream. The foundation's partnership with a local small business development center and a local university also enhances its credibility, generating reputational capital and strengthening its social capital.

Self-Cascading Reflections

We have learned from the chapter that the Red Cross is resilient due to its robust systems and processes for disaster response, including training volunteers, stockpiling supplies, and forming partnerships with like-minded organizations. Drawing from this non-profit organization's success story—and the many other examples of different nonprofit formations in this chapter—let us take a moment to reflect on the following questions:

- What preparedness activities can our organization invest in to ensure we respond quickly and effectively to disasters?
- How can our organization partner with other organizations to access additional resources and expertise during emergencies?
- How can our organization build a solid volunteer base and provide the necessary training and support?
- How can our organization develop an adaptive capacity to respond to changing circumstances and evolving threats?
- What strategies can our organization use to build a strong brand and reputation and to become a trusted partner for governments, donors, and affected communities?

Bend Your Mind!

How many dollars is a dollar? For argument's sake, the dollar I am asking about is a numeraire or value marker, not a physical dollar. It is a unit of measurement of price, not a unit of measurement of value. The dollar could be Renminbi, Ruble, Rial, Baht, Zloty, Balboas, Ringlets, Metical, Quetzal, Drachma, or Dong. All these currencies (despite their innovative names), and all the other currencies of the world, for that matter, are meant to measure the price of an underlying purchase or transaction. In that sense, currency represents value in the eye of the seller, not the purchaser. It satisfies the value for the person selling but not necessarily the person purchasing. While the person selling gets immediate satisfaction from physical or virtual reception of item price, the purchaser only assumes value upon benefiting from the item purchased. This element of time lag is clearly very material, as anything could happen that inhibits assumption of value. Should an inhibitor happen that inhibits assumption of the value, then fairness in the transaction has not been achieved, and the satisfaction score has tilted in favor of the seller.

Now, consider that all transactions are transacted on the assumption that the transacting parties transact at arm's length. There are many issues with this principle. Not all arms are equal in length, and not all palms are equal in size, right? With that being the case, how is it an arm's length trade if one arm is more extended? How is that supposed to be a fair trade if one palm is thicker? The arm length and the palm size are used here pejoratively for power. Power shades and colors are numerous, including the relative affluence of the parties in a trade.

Then, back to the concept/notion of value: does money measure value? Is it really a store of value? Is there anything that can measure value? Because value is not indexable, you cannot measure what you cannot index. Human beings are so many, and each person has a unique perception of value that is not identical to another person.

Then, value is unique. Unlike price, value is indexed through satisfaction of the perceiver, not through the assessment of the giver. Some NGOs seem to have grasped this philosophical notion of value; they are more inclined to measuring the impact of intervention through a real change in the lives of the perceivers, not how much dollars have been spent on the ground. Perception of value and power relativity indicate that fairness and satisfaction from trade are critical and challenging to achieve.

If you happen to have a relatively long arm, why not stretch your arm slightly longer in a typical transaction involving a person with a standard arm?

In other words, if you are buying an item that costs the equivalent of two dollars or paying for a serviceperson that delivered work worth ten dollars, why not stretch your arm by just two or five more dollars, paying them slightly higher than the agreed trade deal? Why do I suggest doing this? Because you are paying for what you have considered as the value you extracted from the deal, and because those two or five extra dollars could represent 50 or 100 dollars in value to the person with the standard arm. Next time you pay for petty services, please do not collect back your little change. It means a lot to them. It also means a lot to you. The internal peace you get from these acts is unmatchable.

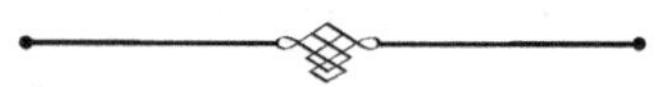

Chapter Ten
LEADING RESILIENCE INDEX

Springboard

n this book, I have defined a crisis as any issue or event that significantly disrupts value creation, either positively or negatively. This is necessary to account for issue management within the overarching organizational resilience strategy. It is also all-encompassing because it equates crisis with disruption and amalgamates a multifaceted lifecycle view. The demarcation between issue and crisis depends on the magnitude and longevity of the disruption. Minor and temporal disruptions are addressed through issue management, while full-fledged crises require crisis resolution measures. The set of policies adopted for issue management and crisis resolution and the level of management and leadership proactiveness determine the speed and direction of organizational post-crisis transformation.

I have also submitted that resilience is becoming the new way of organizational thinking. It is an all-encompassing and overarching organization-wide resilience leadership strategy for value creation in today's volatile, uncertain, complex, ambiguous, and disruptive world. I have further articulated that resilience traits can be acquired and developed using organizational resilience resources, which are then orchestrated. Resilience resource orchestration is a function of resilience resource structuring, bundling, and leveraging. This puts leadership at the center of organizational resilience strategies through the concept of resilience leadership strategies. A clear resilience leadership strategy is foundational to achieving lasting organizational resilience.

Building organizational resilience calls for installing bold leadership that can course-correct and lead the urgently needed transformation through disruption into a new glory of prosperity. Such leaders are fearless but diligent, visionary but tactical, and passionate but level-headed. They play to win. They measure success not by the corporation's size but by value creation. To them, profitability is a means to an end: sustainable growth and resilience. Resilience-oriented leaders emphasize issue management to mitigate the need for crisis management. They would rather self-disrupt than be disrupted. While not always in war-room mode, they are frequently dissatisfied with the status quo, questioning their comfort zones, evaluating the organization's preparedness for surprises, and evolving with the times.

Sustenance of resilience posture begins with realizing that resilience is a journey, not a destination. Therefore, sustaining a resilience posture resides in the continued pursuit of operational resilience excellence. Resilience features throughout their cycle are income stream diversification, improvisation, collaboration, positive reframing, innovation, technological leverage, learning, and organizational transformation. Transformation can help organizations survive and thrive in today's rapidly changing business landscape and is increasingly seen as a critical factor in achieving long-term success. An objective measurement index is necessary to build such an organization.

Accordingly, this chapter presents an LRI as a practical tool for organizations to assess their resilience development metrics. The index helps organizations evaluate and improve their resilience before, during, and after a crisis. The LRI captures resources that can be customized and applied in different contexts. It is an adapted and enhanced version of the items contained in my doctorate dissertation. The items from the doctorate dissertation have been validated following rigorous econometric procedures, including pilot testing and full-scale quantitative and qualitative assessments. The quantitative data were analyzed in SmartPLS version 3 using partial least squares structural equation modeling and standardized root mean square residuals. The qualitative data were gathered using in-depth interviews and document analysis and were analyzed using thematic and content analysis approaches. [49] The LRI contains ten scales, 35 dimensions, and 165 Likert-scale items.

ADMINISTRATION AND MEASUREMENT

The LRI is composed of the following nine scales: issue management scale, within-crisis resilience scale, post-crisis resilience scale, pre-crisis resilience scale, resilience resources scale, resilience orchestration scale, resilience leadership scale, leadership personal resilience scale, and stakeholder perception assessment scale. In addition, it includes two non-scale items: qualitative assessment prompts and resilience buffer ratios. All nine scales of the LRI should be administered anonymously. The process should be managed by dedicated services, such as corporate, research, or human resources. Strict confidentiality should be maintained with zero respondent identification and traceability. An external consultant may be hired to administer and manage the process if an organization cannot maintain strict confidentiality due to logistical issues.

The stakeholder perception assessment is meant to assess an organization's resilience from an external stakeholder perspective. It is critical to provide an objective assessment by outsiders to validate the self-assessment results obtained from internal staff and eliminate biased assessment. Organizations should administer stakeholder perception assessments to creditors, suppliers, customers, the community, and regulatory authorities.

The qualitative assessment evaluates an organization's citizenship, social responsibility, prominence, reputation, competency, culture, and governance. The questions in the scale should be administered to the CEO or board chairperson or their equivalent. It contains 12 prompts: board composition, culture of excellence, digital transformation, dynamism, international orientation, management transition, pace setting, product reputation, strategic commitment, strategic fit, value expression, and work ethics. The prompts are intended to initiate conversation and guide the interview, but the tool administrator has the discretion to customize the prompts in line with the nature of the organization and the perceived concern that needs to be addressed. The interview summary will be converted into a leadership statement and published in the leading resilience report.

The resilience buffer ratios are extracted from accounts and financial reports, including liquidity, solvency, profitability, efficiency, cash flow, and market. "Resilience buffer ratios" is a term coined for this book to refer to the firm's financial performance ratios. Most established commercial corporations publish regular accounts with disclosures, including performance ratios that are either readily available on the account annexures or can be calculated using standard ratio calculation methods. These scales are listed in Table 1.

Table 1. Leading Resilience Index

Scales	Dimensions
Issue Management Scale	Issue Identification, Issue Monitoring, Issue Communication, and Issue Resolution.
Within-crisis Resilience Scale	Positive Reframing, Improvisation, Flexibility, and Collaboration.
Post-crisis Resilience Scale	Adaptability, Recovery, Learning, and Transformation.
Pre-crisis Resilience Scale	Agility, Situational Alertness, and Robustness.
Resilience Resources Scale	Financial Buffer, Reputational Buffer, and Human Capital Buffer.

Resilience Orchestration Scale	Resilience Resource Structuring, Resilience Resource Bundling, and Resilience Resource Leveraging.
Resilience Leadership Scale	Leadership Direction, Leadership Capability, Leadership Quality, and Leadership Adequacy.
Leadership Personal Resilience Scale	Adversity Intelligence, Practical Intelligence, Social Intelligence, Emotional Intelligence, and Spiritual Intelligence.
Stakeholder Perception Assessment Scale	Citizenship Perception, Collaboration Perception, Communication Perception, Competency Perception, and Reputation Perception.
Qualitative Assessment Prompts	Board Composition, Culture of Excellence, Digital Transformation, Dynamism, International Presence, Management Transition, Pace Setting, Product Reputation, Strategic Commitment, Strategic Fit, Value Expression, and Work Ethics.
Resilience Buffer Ratios	Liquidity, Solvency, Profitability, Efficiency, Cash Flow, and Market.

RESPONSE RECORDING

The scales, dimensions, and questions measure the organization's LRI. The LRI is a single ratio calculated as a composite average of all the indices. However, the tool can also be used for partial assessment to address specific issues or concerns. Only the targeted question entries in the targeted dimension or scale are administered to the relevant respondents.

Apart from the qualitative assessment prompts and resilience score buffer ratios, all nine indices are constructed and measured on a five-point Likert scale with two mutually non-exclusive measurement scale options adopted for convenience and consistency: "agree-disagree" and "never-continually." Hence, questions containing verbs such as "we treat client feedback with deserved attention" are answered on a "never-continually" scale, and questions containing adjectives such as "our leaders are vigilant" are answered on an "agree-disagree" scale.[347] Each question in the nine scales provides five answer options: "1" indicates "strongly disagree" or "never," "2" indicates "disagree" or "rarely," "3" indicates "neutral" or "sometimes," "4" indicates "agree" or "mostly," and "5" indicates "strongly agree" or "continuously," as illustrated in Table 2.

Table 2. Likert-Scale Scoring Options

Answers	Option One	Option Two
1	Strongly Disagree	Never
2	Disagree	Rarely
3	Neutral	Sometimes
4	Agree	Mostly
5	Strongly Agree	Continuously

SCORING PROCEDURE

Once the answers are recorded, an arithmetic mean of question scores will be calculated. The aggregate of the arithmetic means of question scores under each dimension will measure that dimension. Similarly, the scale will aggregate the arithmetic means of all the dimensions constituting that scale. Finally, the index will be calculated as an aggregate of all the scales multiplied by 100. Similarly, a percentage score can be applied to a single dimension or scale. Blank responses should be ignored as a best practice. The aggregation levels, measurement, and calculation of the various score levels are listed in Table 3.

Table 3. Scoring Levels and Computation

Item	Aggregation Level	Measurement	Calculation
Likert Items	Total Respondent Scores	Likert Scale	1 to 5
Dimensions	Total Questions	Mean Score	The sum of respondent scores divided by the number of questions
Scales	Total Dimensions	Composite Score	The sum of dimensions divided by the number of dimensions
Index	Total Scales	Aggregate Score	The sum of scales divided by the number of scales and multiplied by 100

GRADING AND INTERPRETATION

Based on the grading outcome of the LRI, organizations are classified into five categories, as shown in Table 4. First, organizations scoring 20 percent and below are graded as "Struggling." Second, organizations scoring between 21 and 40 percent are graded as "Surviving." Third, organizations scoring between 41 and 60 percent are graded as "Adapting." Fourth, organizations scoring between 61 and 80 percent are graded as "Emerging." Finally, organizations scoring 81 percent or more are graded as "Thriving."

The qualitative assessment prompts and resilience buffer ratios validate the results of the nine scales. The qualitative assessment assesses an organization's outlook based on what its leadership believes and plans to achieve. The qualitative assessment is assigned three scores: "Negative," "Neutral," and "Positive." A negative assessment downgrades an organization's outlook by one notch, a neutral assessment keeps its outlook without change, and a positive assessment upgrades its outlook to the immediate upper notch. If the index results in an organization being graded as "Struggling," the qualitative assessment will either be "Neutral" or "Positive" since "Struggling" represents the bottom of the grading echelon. A neutral qualitative assessment keeps the organization's outlook at "Struggling." A positive qualitative assessment upgrades it to "Surviving." Likewise, if the organization is graded "Thriving" based on the index, a negative qualitative assessment will move it to "Emerging." A neutral qualitative assessment keeps it at "Thriving" since thriving represents the top grading. The gradings and interpretations are listed in Table 4.

Table 4. LRI Interpretation

Score	Ratio	Grading	Qualitative Assessment	Revised Grading
1	1%-20%	Struggling	Neutral Positive	Neutral Surviving
2	21%-40%	Surviving	Negative Neutral Positive	Struggling Neutral Adapting
3	41%-60%	Adapting	Negative Neutral Positive	Surviving Neutral Emerging
4	61%-80%	Emerging	Negative Neutral Positive	Adapting Neutral Thriving
5	81%-100%	Thriving	Negative Neutral	Emerging Neutral

LRI MEASUREMENT TABLES

Table 5. Issue Management Scale

Codes	Questions	Dimensions	Scores
IsM1	We engage relevant stakeholders on issues affecting our organization.	Issue Communication	
IsM2	Our leadership provides updates on pertinent issues affecting us.		
IsM3	We have established collaborative relationships across the industry.		
IsM4	We use group email or social media alerts to communicate pertinent matters.		
IsM5	We get to know serious issues affecting our organization through official internal channels.		
IsM6	We rely on data and analytical tools to assess our preparedness.	Issue Identification	
IsM7	We employ a systematic approach to identifying operational weaknesses.		
IsM8	We have a secure and reliable channel where staff can communicate issues to management.		
IsM9	We proactively protect our organization from issues arising within our industry or neighborhood.		
IsM10	We treat client feedback with deserved attention.		

IsM11	We have a policy for reporting issues to the appropriate levels of supervision.		
IsM12	Our organization actively monitors and tracks potential issues that will likely impact our operations.		
IsM13	We have an internal process of reporting and escalating issues to the appropriate managerial levels.	Issue Monitoring	
IsM14	Our organization prioritizes and addresses issues based on their potential impact on the business.		
IsM15	We have a team that monitors potential issues impacting our performance.		
IsM16	When performance-related issues arise, we take steps to address them.		
IsM17	We are keen to address issues impacting our operations.		
IsM18	We prioritize dealing with issues based on their potential impact.	Issue Resolution	
IsM19	We document issue-resolution methods and the lessons learned.		
IsM20	We evaluate the effectiveness of our issue-resolution strategies.		

Table 6. Within-crisis Resilience Scale

Codes	Questions	Dimensions	Scores
WcR1	Our team members are diverse and creative.	Collaboration	
WcR2	Our organization fosters a culture of trust.		
WcR3	We work as a team to achieve common objectives.		
WcR4	We cultivate a culture of inclusiveness and diversity.		
WcR5	We encourage collaboration and teamwork.		
WcR6	Our rigidity inhibits our ability to respond to challenges.	Flexibility	
WcR7	We are a flexible organization that is constantly evolving.		
WcR8	We pivot to new products or services.		
WcR9	We are persistently in search of the best approaches to business.		
WcR10	We can adapt to new ways of doing business.		

WcR11	Our leaders can make discretionary decisions without fear.	Improvisation	
WcR12	Our organization can generate creative solutions to unexpected challenges quickly.		
WcR13	Our organization has a culture of experimentation and learning from failures.		
WcR14	Our organization can make decisions and take action with limited information.		
WcR15	Our organization fosters an environment of trust where employees can use their best judgment and make independent decisions.		
WcR16	We can focus on the positive aspects of challenging situations.	Positive Reframing	
WcR17	We see an opportunity in every challenge we face.		
WcR18	We maintain hope and possibility, even in the face of significant challenges.		
WcR19	Out organizational leaders project optimism in challenging situations.		
WcR20	We can demonstrate optimism in the face of challenges.		

Table 7. Post-crisis Resilience Scale

Codes	Questions	Dimensions	Scores
PcR1	We can reassess our performance targets when needed.	Adaptability	
PcR2	We are aligned with the best industry and market practices.		
PcR3	We adjust our strategies to remain relevant and practical.		
PcR4	Our organization can successfully navigate complex situations.		
PcR5	We adapt to changing conditions with open-mindedness.		
PcR6	We look at the root cause of problems to understand them.	Learning	
PcR7	We share best practices and knowledge across our teams.		
PcR8	We share knowledge across our organization to promote learning.		
PcR9	We collaborate with our industry peers to cross-fertilize knowledge and growth.		
PcR10	Our leaders encourage a mindset of growth.		

PcR11	We can restore our normalcy with relative ease whenever we encounter operational disruptions.	Recovery	
PcR12	We can activate contingency plans to continue operating in disruption.		
PcR13	Our organization has a post-crisis recovery plan.		
PcR14	We have a decentralized and cloud-based data recovery platform.		
PcR15	We have established an effective disaster recovery plan.		
PcR16	My colleagues can help me overcome challenges.	Transformation	
PcR17	We perceive change as an opportunity to grow and transform.		
PcR18	We can overcome challenges and emerge with renewed purpose and direction.		
PcR19	Staff can connect with their leaders on social networks.		
PcR20	Challenges are seen as an opportunity to excel.		

Table 8. Pre-crisis Resilience Scale

Codes	Questions	Dimensions	Scores
PrR1	We can transition from routine business operations to crisis management.	Agility	
PrR2	We encourage experimentation and exploration.		
PrR3	Our leaders are vigilant.		
PrR4	We respond proactively to emerging threats and challenges.		
PrR5	For each plan that we develop, we have a plan B.		
PrR6	Our leaders can communicate bad news diligently but transparently.	Situational Alertness	
PrR7	Our staff can easily talk to management about their concerns.		
PrR8	We understand what situational alertness means to our business.		
PrR9	We are concerned with what is happening beyond our walls.		
PrR10	Our customers perceive our organization as a trustworthy partner.		

Codes	Questions	Dimensions	Scores
PrR11	Our business continuity plan is current and effective.	Robustness	
PrR12	We have a decision-making system that is not centrally controlled.		
PrR13	We have a reliable, cloud-based data management system.		
PrR14	We can adapt and adjust seamlessly to any situation.		
PrR15	Our shareholders are happy with our performance.		

Table 9. Resilience Resource Scale

Codes	Questions	Dimensions	Scores
ReR1	Our suppliers and creditors trust us because we honor our contractual obligations easily.	Financial Buffer	
ReR2	Our business has grown thanks to our efficient financial resources management policy.		
ReR3	Financial return figures prominently in our investment decisions.		
ReR4	Our growth has primarily been organic.		
ReR5	We have committed shareholders who believe in the future of our business.		

ReR6	Our staff possesses skills commensurate with their assigned responsibilities.	Human Capital Buffer	
ReR7	We have a talent pool suited to sustain our succession planning.		
ReR8	Our training programs are suited for our performance sustainability.		
ReR9	Our employees are committed to ethical and responsible business practices.		
ReR10	We are an inclusive and culturally tolerant organization.		
ReR11	We enjoy strong shareholder support.	Reputational Buffer	
ReR12	We can leverage our organizational reputation to negotiate favorable terms.		
ReR13	We can sustain our relevance in the marketplace for years ahead.		
ReR14	We cross-fertilize and share learning across our organization.		
ReR15	Part of our business growth is due to satisfied customer referrals.		

Table 10. Resilience Resource Orchestration Scale

Codes	Questions	Dimensions	Scores
RrO1	We apply procedures for asset acquisition and disposal.	Resilience Resource Bundling	
RrO2	We are considered leaders in product and process innovation.		
RrO3	We are capable of developing new products and services to maintain our growth.		
RrO4	Innovative and pioneering ideas are encouraged and rewarded in our organization.		
RrO5	We have consistently maintained a high return on investment.		
RrO6	Our talent pool is diverse and versatile.	Resilience Resource Leveraging	
RrO7	Our resource management strategy is aligned with our growth.		
RrO8	We encourage our staff to innovate.		
RrO9	We use our assets and capabilities diligently to support our growth.		
RrO10	Our growth is driven by how we employ our existing resources.		

RrO11	We adopt state-of-the-art technology in our core operations.		
RrO12	Our investment strategy is geared toward sustainable growth.		
RrO13	We look to improve and maximize the use of existing assets before acquiring new ones.	Resilience Resource Structuring	
RrO14	We prioritize investment in research and development to bring new ideas and products into the market.		
RrO15	Operational weaknesses are a concern for our management.		

Table 11. Resilience Leadership Scale

Codes	Questions	Dimensions	Scores
RlS1	Our organization's ethical conduct is well-recognized.	Leadership Capability	
RlS2	Our leaders can adapt to new ways of doing business.		
RlS3	Our leaders are aware and tolerant of cultural diversity.		
RlS4	Our leadership team understands the issues facing our organization.		
RlS5	Our leaders do not hesitate to make tough choices.		
RlS6	We espouse our vision in all that we do.	Leadership Direction	
RlS7	I feel proud to be part of this organization.		
RlS8	Our mission statement inspires us to persevere and perform.		
RlS9	Our mission statement guides our focus on critical deliverables.		
RlS10	Our core values inspire positive employee morale.		

RIS11	Our leaders can hold themselves accountable.	Leadership Quality	
RIS12	Our management promotes work-life balance.		
RIS13	Our customers are the center of our attention.		
RIS14	Our leaders have a creative mindset.		
RIS15	We enjoy social benefits and wellbeing support.		
RIS16	Our organization is mapped out clearly, and each position and role is defined.	Leadership Adequacy	
RIS17	Our hiring policy is linked to our succession planning.		
RIS18	More people are hired than those who are leaving.		
RIS19	I believe I can get promoted if I work hard.		
RIS20	Our vacant leadership positions are filled with relative ease.		

Table 12. Leadership Personal Resilience Scale

Codes	Questions	Dimensions	Scores
LpR1	Setbacks provide me with an opportunity for personal growth.	Adversity Intelligence	
LpR2	I am open to feedback and willing to learn from my mistakes.		
LpR3	I can maintain a positive attitude even in challenging circumstances.		
LpR4	I can remain calm and composed under pressure.		
LpR5	I am willing to experiment with new things.		
LpR6	I can sympathize with others and understand their perspective.	Emotional Intelligence	
LpR7	I can adapt my communication style to suit different audiences.		
LpR8	I am aware of my emotional triggers and can manage them.		
LpR9	I can recognize when others are experiencing a range of emotions.		
LpR10	I can express empathy toward others.		

LpR11	I am open to constructive criticism.	Practical Intelligence	
LpR12	I can see the big picture and understand the context of challenging situations.		
LpR13	I can recognize and address my biases.		
LpR14	I can manage my time and resources under constraints.		
LpR15	I am not afraid to delegate tasks and responsibilities.		
LpR16	I can effectively communicate with others.	Social Intelligence	
LpR17	I can influence others to achieve desired outcomes.		
LpR18	I can give others constructive feedback without offending them.		
LpR19	I can handle criticism without becoming defensive or emotional.		
LpR20	I often use humor to help alleviate stress.		
LpR21	I can use my spiritual beliefs to guide my decision-making.	Spiritual Intelligence	
LpR22	I always believe that tomorrow could be better.		
LpR23	I can find meaning in positive and negative experiences in life.		
LpR24	I respect the spiritual beliefs of others, even if they differ from mine.		
LpR25	I can express gratitude no matter how small it may be.		

Table 13. Stakeholder Perception Assessment Scale

Codes	Questions	Dimensions	Scores
SpA1	The organization is alert to its operating environment.	Citizenship	
SpA2	The organization promotes charitable endeavors.		
SpA3	The organization is a responsible and compliant corporate citizen.		
SpA4	The organization can resolve issues through mutual understanding.	Collaboration	
SpA5	The organization can collaborate to achieve win-win results.		
SpA6	The organization can work with different stakeholder groups.		
SpA7	The organization communicates promptly and transparently.	Communication	
SpA8	The organization figures prominently in charitable and social activities.		
SpA9	The presence of this organization has a positive impact on our community.		

SpA10	Organizational leadership exemplifies confidence and trust.	Competency	
SpA11	The organization has an approach to handling disputes.		
SpA12	The organization addresses stakeholder concerns satisfactorily.		
SpA13	People mention this organization in positive contexts most of the time.	Reputation	
SpA14	I rank this organization in the top five regarding its positive impact.		
SpA15	I would not hesitate to recommend the products and services of this organization to other customers.		

Table 14. Qualitative Assessment Prompts

Code	Assessment Items	Prompts
QaP1	Board composition	How is the organization's board diversity, inclusion, gender balance, and industry knowledge?
QaP2	Culture of excellence	How reputable is the organization in terms of product and service excellence?
QaP3	Digital transformation	What is the organization's level of investment in technology and digital transformation?
QaP4	Dynamism	How dynamic is the organization's senior management, particularly the C-suite?
QaP5	Global perspective	Does the organization think global or have global relevance?
QaP6	Management transition	What is the senior management turnover and internal reshuffling frequency?
QaP7	Pace setting	Does the organization set a growth pace in the industry?
QaP8	Product reputation	How often does the organization upgrade its product and service offerings?
QaP9	Strategic commitment	How committed is the organization to its mandate, objectives, and environment?
QaP10	Strategic fit	How do an organization's operations fit into its stated strategy, vision, and mission?
QaP11	Value expression	What is the single most critical value that the organization proposes and promotes?
QaP12	Work ethics	Is the organization known to promote a conducive work environment?

Table 15. Resilience Buffer Ratios

Ratios	Lower Threshold (per industry)	Medium Threshold (per industry)	Upper Threshold (per industry)
Liquidity			
Solvency			
Profitability			
Efficiency			
Cash Flow			
Market			

REFERENCES

1   **9/11 Commission**. 2004. *The 9/11 Commission Report: Final Report of the National Commission on Terrorist Attacks Upon the United States (9/11 Report)*. US. https://www.govinfo.gov/app/details/GPO-911REPORT

2   **Roberts, B.W.** 2009. The macroeconomic impacts of the 9/11 attack: evidence from real-time forecasting. *Peace Economics, Peace Science and Public Policy*, 15(2): 341-367. https://doi.org/10.2202/1554-8597.1166

3   **World Health Organization** 2006. *The world health report 2006: Working together for health*. World Health Organization.

4   **Waltham, T.** 2005. The Asian Tsunami disaster, December 2004. *Geology Today*, 21(1): 22-26. https://doi.org/10.1111/j.1365-2451.2005.00495.x

5   **Kazmi, Z.A. & Sodangi, M.** 2019. The 2005 Kashmir Earthquake—devastation of infrastructures. *Proceedings of the Institution of Civil Engineers-Structures and Buildings*, 172(7): 490-501. https://doi.org/10.1680/jstbu.17.00069

6   **Davis, T., Rogers, H., Shays, C., Bonilla, H., Buyer, S., Myrick, S., Thornberry, M. *et al.*** 2006. *A failure of initiative: Final report of the select bipartisan committee to investigate the preparation for and response to Hurricane Katrina*. Washington. https://www.nrc.gov/docs/ML1209/ML12093A081.pdf

7   **Stulz, R.M.** 2010. Credit default swaps and the credit crisis. *Journal of Economic Perspectives*, 24(1): 73-92. https://doi.org/10.1257/jep.24.1.73

8   **Barrell, R. & Davis, E.P.** 2008. The evolution of the financial crisis of 2007-8. *National Institute economic review,* 206(1): 5-14. https://doi.org/10.1177/0027950108099838

9   **Yom, S.** 2015. The Arab Spring: One region, several puzzles, and many explanations. *Government and Opposition,* 50(4): 682-704. https://doi.org/10.1017/gov.2015.19

10   **Huber, C., Finelli, L. & Stevens, W.** 2018. The economic and social burden of the 2014 Ebola outbreak in West Africa. *J Infect Dis,* 218(suppl_5): S698-S704. https://doi.org/10.1093/infdis/jiy213

11   **Drachal, K. & Gonzalez Cortes, D.** 2022. Estimation of lockdowns' impact on well-being in selected countries: An application of novel bayesian methods and Google search queries data. *Int J Environ Res Public Health,* 20(1): 421. https://doi.org/10.3390/ijerph20010421

12   **Tabar, M., Gluck, J., Goyal, A., Jiang, F., Morr, D., Kehs, A., Lee, D., Hughes, D.P. & Yadav, A.** 2021. A plan for tackling the locust crisis in east Africa: harnessing spatiotemporal deep models for locust movement forecasting. Conference presentation at Proceedings of the 27th ACM SIGKDD Conference on Knowledge Discovery & Data Mining. August 14–18, 2021. https://doi.org/10.1145

13   **Al-Hajj, S., Dhaini, H.R., Mondello, S., Kaafarani, H., Kobeissy, F. & DePalma, R.G.** 2021. Beirut ammonium nitrate blast: analysis, review, and recommendations. *Frontiers in public health,* 9. https://doi.org/10.3389/fpubh.2021.657996

14   **Raga, S. & Pettinotti, L.** 2022. *Economic vulnerability to the Russia–Ukraine war: Which low- and middle-income countries are most vulnerable? Outward Direct Investment Emerging Analysis. London.* http://cdn-odi-production.s3-website-eu-west-1.amazonaws.com/media/documents/1Updated_Final_-_Economic_vulnerability_to_the_RussiaUkraine_War-Raga_and_Pett_nR2sBzE.pdf

15   **Ruta, M.** 2022. The impact of the war in Ukraine on global trade and investment. Washington, DC. https://documents1.worldbank.org/curated/en/099750104252216595/pdf/IDU0008eed66007300452c0beb208e8903183c39.pdf

16 **Pharaoh, C.D.** 2018 An investigation into what the management competencies are during a time of crisis: A university stakeholder perspective. South Africa University of the Western Cape. Magister Commercii - MCom (Business and Finance). http://hdl.handle.net/11394/6694

17 **Jaques, T.** 2007. Issue management and crisis management: An integrated, non-linear, relational construct. *Public relations review,* 33(2): 147-157. https://doi.org/10.1016/j.pubrev.2007.02.001

18 **Koivisto, J.** 2012 Chronic crisis: A landscape analysis of newspapers. Available at: https://trepo.tuni.fi/handle/10024/83619

19 **Harrison, G.** 2005 Communication strategies as a basis for crisis management including use of the internet as a delivery platform. USA. Georgia State University. Unpublished Doctorate Dissertation.

20 **Mehan, A. & Jansen, M.** 2020. *Beirut Blast: A port city in crisis.* https://www.portcityfutures.nl/news/beirut-blast-a-port-city-in-crisis

21 **Rosen, R.E.** 2002. Risk management and corporate governance: The case of Enron. *Conn. L. Rev.,* 35: 1157. Available at SSRN: https://ssrn.com/abstract=468168

22 **McKibbin, W.J. & Stoeckel, A.** 2010. The global financial crisis: Causes and consequences. *Asian Economic Papers,* 9(1): 54-86. https://doi.org/10.1162/asep.2010.9.1.54

23 **Jung, J.C. & Sharon, E.** 2019. The Volkswagen emissions scandal and its aftermath. *Global Business and Organizational Excellence,* 38(4): 6-15. https://doi.org/10.1002/joe.21930

24 **Rollin, J.** *FIFA corruption scandal,* Encyclopedia Britannica. https://www.britannica.com/event/2015-FIFA-corruption-scandal

25 **Danylchuk, K., Stegink, J. & Lebel, K.** 2016. Doping scandals in professional cycling: impact on primary team sponsor's stock return. *International journal of sports marketing and sponsorship,* 17(1): 37-55. https://doi.org/10.1108/IJSMS-02-2016-003

26 **Pauli, B.J.** 2020. The Flint water crisis. *Wiley Interdisciplinary Reviews: Water,* 7(3): e1420. https://doi.org/10.1002/wat2.1420

27   **Watt, R.** 2017. Grenfell Tower fire–a tragic case study in health inequalities. *British dental journal,* 223(7): 478-480. https://doi.org/10.1038/sj.bdj.2017.785

28   **Griffin, A.** 2014. *Crisis, issues and reputation management.* Kogan Page Publishers.

29   **Lauge, A., Sarriegi, J.M. & Torres, J.M.** 2009. The dynamics of crisis lifecycle for emergency management. Conference presentation at The 27th International Conference of the System Dynamics Society. University of Navarra,. https://proceedings.systemdynamics.org/2009/proceed/papers/P1112.pdf

30   **Benoit, W.L.** 2018. Crisis and image repair at United Airlines: Fly the unfriendly skies. *Journal of International Crisis and Risk Communication Research,* 1(1): 11-26. https://doi.org/10.30658/jicrcr.1.1.2

31   **Holt, M., Campbell, R.J. & Nikitin, M.B.** 2012. Fukushima nuclear disaster. Congressional Research Service Washington, DC, USA.

32   **Sweeney, K., Schramm-Possinger, M., Gregg, E.A. & Stranahan, H.** 2016. Predicting consumer commitment: A case study of the NFL and ray rice. *Case Studies in Sport Management,* 5(1): 89-94. https://doi.org/10.1123/cssm.2015-0048

33   **Lins, K.V., Roth, L., Servaes, H. & Tamayo, A.** 2021. Sexism, culture, and firm value: evidence from the Harvey Weinstein scandal and the MeToo movement. *University of Alberta School of Business Research Paper No. 2019-509.* https://doi.org/10.2139/ssrn.3458312

34   **Bennett, N. & Lemoine, G.J.** 2014. What a difference a word makes: Understanding threats to performance in a VUCA world. *Business Horizons,* 57(3): 311-317. https://doi.org/10.4236/psych.2012.33041

35   **Ramakrishnan, R.** 2021. Leading in a VUCA World. *Ushus Journal of Business Management,* 20(1): 89-111. https://doi.org/10.12725/ujbm.54.5

36   **Canyon, D.K.** 2020. *Definitions in crisis management and crisis leadership.* Honolulu. Available at: https://dkiapcss.edu/nexus_articles/definitions-in-crisis-management-and-crisis-leadership/

37 **Alvi, M.F., Gupta, S. & Barooah, P.** 2022. *Assessing the impact of COVID-19 on rural women and men in Dang District, Nepal.* Vol. 7. Intl Food Policy Res Inst.

38 **Barretto Briso, C. & Phillips, T.** 2020. Brazil gangs impose strict curfews to slow coronavirus spread. *The Guardian,* 25. https://www.theguardian.com/world/2020/mar/25/brazil-rio-gangs-coronavirus

39 **Shupler, M., Mwitari, J., Gohole, A., de Cuevas, R.A., Puzzolo, E., Čukić, I., Nix, E. & Pope, D.** 2021. COVID-19 impacts on household energy & food security in a Kenyan informal settlement: The need for integrated approaches to the SDGs. *Renewable and Sustainable Energy Reviews,* 144: 111018. https://doi.org/10.1016/j.rser.2021.111018

40 **Krawczyńska-Zaucha, T.** 2019. A new paradigm of management and leadership in the VUCA world. *Zeszyty Naukowe. Organizacja i Zarządzanie/Politechnika Śląska,* (141): 221-230. https://doi.org/10.29119/1641-3466.2019.141.16

41 **Labaš, D., Pršir, A. & Puškar, J.** 2018. Evolving crisis management-current jobs and required employee's skills and characteristics analysis. Conference presentation at 6th International OFEL Conference on Governance, Management and Entrepreneurship. April 13th-14th, 2018, Dubrovnik, Croatia. Zagreb: Governance Research and Development Centre. https://www.econstor.eu/bitstream/10419/180012/1/ofel-2018-p524-582.pdf

42 **Calabrese, R., Cowling, M. & Liu, W.** 2022. Understanding the dynamics of UK Covid-19 SME financing. *British Journal of Management,* 33(2): 657-677. https://doi.org/10.1111/1467-8551.12576

43 **Fernandes, F.S.M.S.** 2021 Intercontinental hotels group-time to check-in? analysis of one of the biggest hotel players in times of a global pandemic. Universidade Nova de Lisboa. MBA. http://hdl.handle.net/10362/122740

44 **Dumbravă, V. & Iacob, V.-S.** 2013. UUsing Probability-Impact Matrix in Analysis and Risk Assessment Projects. Descrierea CIP/Description of CIP-Biblioteca Nationala a

Romaniei Conferinta Internationala Educatie si Creativitate pentru o Societate Bazata pe Cuno-astere-Stiinte Economice, 42. *Open Access Library Journal,* 42. https://www.scirp.org/ (S(351jmbntvnsjt1aadkozje))/reference/referencespapers. aspx?referenceid=2179230

45   **Kassem, M., Khoiry, M.A. & Hamzah, N.** 2020. Using probability impact matrix (PIM) in analyzing risk factors affecting the success of oil and gas construction projects in Yemen. *International Journal of Energy Sector Management,* 14(3): 527-546. https://doi.org/10.1108/IJESM-03-2019-0011

46   **Valackienė, A. & Virbickaitė, R.** 2011. Conceptualization of crisis situation in a company. *Journal of Business Economics and Management,* 12(2): 317-331. https://doi.org/10.3846/1611169 9.2011.575192

47   **Hacker, J., vom Brocke, J., Handali, J., Otto, M. & Schneider, J.** 2020. Virtually in this together—how web-conferencing systems enabled a new virtual togetherness during the COVID-19 crisis. *European Journal of Information Systems,* 29(5): 563-584. https://doi.org/10.1080/0960085X.2020.1814680

48   **Kersan-Skabic, I.** 2022. The COVID-19 pandemic and the internationalization of production: A review of the literature. *Dev Policy Rev,* 40(2): e12560. https://doi.org/10.1111/dpr.12560

49   **Ahmed, E.** 2022 Leadership strategy, resource orchestration, firm size, and organizational resilience among listed banks in Kenya. Nairobi, Kenya. Pan Africa Christian University. Unpublished Doctorate Dissertation.

50   **Sabahi, S. & Parast, M.M.** 2019. Firm innovation and supply chain resilience: a dynamic capability perspective. *International Journal of Logistics Research and Applications,* 23(3): 254-269. https://doi.org/10.1080/13675567.2019.1683522

51   **Ahmed, E., Kilika, J. & Gekenia, C.** 2022. Strategy-induced organisational resilience through dynamic resource orchestration: Perspectives of former Kenyan bankers. *International Journal of Research in Business and Social Science (2147-4478),* 11(2): 92-103. https://doi.org/10.20525/ijrbs.v11i2.1633

52 **Venugopal, A., Vaid, N. & Bowman, S.J.** 2021. Outstanding, yet redundant? After all, you may be another Choluteca Bridge! *Seminars in Orthodontics,* 27(1): 53-56. https://doi.org/10.1053/j.sodo.2021.03.007

53 **Reeves, M., Love, C. & Tillmanns, P.** 2012. Your strategy needs a strategy. *Harvard Business Review,* 90(9): 76-83. https://hbr.org/2012/09/your-strategy-needs-a-strategy

54 **Bock, F., Hellweg, M., Lube, M.-M. & Mühlhäuser, H.** 1998. A strategy for supporting innovation and growth in times of high uncertainty. *PRISM-Cambridge Massachusetts*: 21-34. https://www.adlittle.com/sites/default/files/prism/1998_q3_07-13.pdf

55 **Mintzberg, H., Ahlstrand, B. & Lampel, J.** 2008. *Strategy bites back! It is far more and less than you have ever imagined.* Prentice Hall, New York.

56 **Franklin, P.** 2001. Is strategy still relevant? *Strategic change,* 10(4): 183-188. https://doi.org/10.1002/jsc.551

57 **Narikae, P. & Lewa, P.** 2017. The origins and development of strategic management "knowledge": A historical perspective. *European Journal of Business and Strategic Management,* 2(6): 1-19. https://www.iprjb.org/

58 **Khan, M. & Khalique, M.** 2014. Strategic planning and reality of external environment of organizations in contemporary business environments. *Business Management and Strategy,* 5(2). https://doi.org/10.5296/bms.v5i2.6794

59 **Meyer, A.D., Brooks, G.R. & Goes, J.B.** 1990. Environmental jolts and industry revolutions: Organizational responses to discontinuous change. *Strategic management journal,* 11(4): 93-110. https://onlinelibrary.wiley.com/journal/10970266

60 **Cooper, M.** 2019. The Rise and Fall of Commodore. *ITNOW,* 61(3): 16-19. https://doi.org/10.1093/itnow/bwz063

61 **Bruijl, G.** 2018. The Relevance of Porter's Five Forces in Today's Innovative and Changing Business Environment. *SSRN Electronic Journal.* https://doi.org/10.2139/ssrn.3192207

62 **Southern University at New Orleans** 2011. *Strategic planning handbook and managers implementation tools.* New Orleans, Southern University at New Orleans.

63   **Mandel, D.R.P.** 2020 Strategic planning constraints within a fast pace changing organizational context. Lisbon, Portugal. European University. Master's Thesis. http://hdl.handle.net/10400.26/33250

64   **Beinhocker, E.D. & Kaplan, S.** 2002. Tired of strategic planning. *The McKinsey Quarterly,* 2(Special Edition): 48-57. https://www.mckinsey.com/

65   **Groh, M.** 2014. Strategic management in times of crisis. *American Journal of Economics and Business Administration,* 6(2): 49.57. https://doi.org/10.3844/ajebasp.2014

66   **Morgan, G.** 2006. *Images of organisation.* CA, Sage Publicatinos Inc.

67   **Teece, D.J.** 2018. Dynamic capabilities as (workable) management systems theory. *Journal of Management & Organization,* 24(3): 359-368. https://doi.org/10.1017/jmo.2017.75

68   **Duchek, S.** 2019. Organizational resilience: a capability-based conceptualization. *Business Research,* 13(1): 215-246. https://doi.org/10.1007/s40685-019-0085-7

69   **Ahmed, E., Kilika, J. & Gakenia, C.** 2021. The conceptualization of dynamic resource orchestration framework as an anchor for organizational resilience. *International Journal of Research in Business and Social Science (2147- 4478),* 10(7): 53-61. https://doi.org/10.20525/ijrbs.v10i7.1419

70   **Bakshi, C.V.** 2017. *The forward-looking manager in a VUCA world.* SAGE Publishing India.

71   **Lampropoulos, A.** 2022. Towards urban and structural resilience in earthquake engineering. pp. 273-273. Taylor & Francis.

72   **Perry, J.M., Modesti, C., Nicolais, C., Talamo, A. & Nicolais, G.** 2022. The multifaceted nature of the response to adversity in an Italian sample of refugee community leaders. *J Trauma Stress,* 35(2): 362-374. https://doi.org/10.1002/jts.22745

73   **Masten, A.S.** 2019. Resilience from a developmental systems perspective. *World Psychiatry,* 18(1): 101-102. https://doi.org/10.1002/wps.20591

74   **Ramdani, B., Binsaif, A., Boukrami, E. & Guermat, C.** 2022. Business models innovation in investment banks: a

resilience perspective. *Asia Pacific Journal of Management,* 39(1): 51-78. https://doi.org/10.1007/s10490-020-09723-z

75 **McManus, S., Seville, E., Brunsdon, D. & Vargo, J.** 2007. Resilience management: a framework for assessing and improving the resilience of organisations. *Resilient Organisations Research Report University of Canterbury. Civil and Natural Resources Engineering.* https://ir.canterbury.ac.nz/handle/10092/2810

76 **Heng, G.** 2015. Business continuity management planning methodology. *International journal of disaster recovery and business continuity,* 6(1): 9-16. https://doi.org/10.14257/ijdrbc.2015.6.02

77 **Mamun, S., Hansen, J.K. & Roni, M.S.** 2020. Supply, operational, and market risk reduction opportunities: Managing risk at a cellulosic biorefinery. *Renewable and Sustainable Energy Reviews,* 121. https://doi.org/10.1016/j.rser.2019.109677

78 **Mittal, V. & Raman, T.** 2021. Examining the determinants and consequences of financial constraints faced by Micro, Small and Medium Enterprises' owners. *World Journal of Entrepreneurship, Management and Sustainable Development,* 17(3): 560-581. https://doi.org/10.1108/WJEMSD-07-2020-0089

79 **Ahmed, E., Kilika, J. & Gakenia, C.** 2021. Progressive convergent definition and conceptualization of organizational resilience: A model development. *International Journal of Organizational Leadership,* 10(4): 385-400. https://doi.org/10.33844/ijol.2021.60599

80 **Tomislav, K.** 2018. The concept of sustainable development: From its beginning to the contemporary issues. *Zagreb International Review of Economics & Business,* 21(1): 67-94. https://doi.org/10.2478/zireb-2018-0005

81 **Antoniades, A., Widiarto, I. & Antonarakis, A.S.** 2020. Financial crises and the attainment of the SDGs: an adjusted multidimensional poverty approach. *Sustainability Science,* 15(6): 1683-1698. https://doi.org/10.1007/s11625-019-00771-z

82 **Caparusso, J.C., Chen, Y., Dattels, P., Goel, R. & Hiebert, P.** 2019. *Post-crisis changes in global bank business models: a new taxonomy.* International Monetary Fund.

83 **Tarullo, D.K.** 2019. Financial regulation: Still unsettled a decade after the crisis. *Journal of Economic Perspectives,* 33(1): 61-80. https://doi.org/10.1257/jep.33.1.61

84 **Gudmundsson, R., Ngoka-Kisinguh, K. & Odongo, M.** 2013. *The role of capital requirements on bank competition and stability: The case of the Kenyan banking industry.* Nairobi. https://www.kba.co.ke/wp-content/uploads/2022/05/Working_Paper_WPS_05_122.pdf

85 **Carletti, E., Claessens, S., Fatás, A. & Vives, X.** 2020. *Post-Covid-19 World.* Centre for Economic Policy Research.

86 **Mateev, M., Tariq, M.U. & Sahyouni, A.** 2021. Competition, capital growth and risk-taking in emerging markets: Policy implications for banking sector stability during COVID-19 pandemic. *Plos one,* 16(6): e0253803. https://doi.org/10.1371/journal.pone.0253803

87 **Kring, D.A.** 2013. Chelyabinsk air burst: A dramatic illustration of a Near-Earth Asteroid impact. *Lunar and Planetary Information Bulletin,* 133: 1-5. www.lpi.usra.edu/lpib

88 **Gladysheva, O.** 2018. Meteorite chelyabinsk: Features of destruction. *Natural Science,* 10(11): 430-435. https://doi.org/10.4236/ns.2018.1011042

89 **Miller, S.D., Straka III, W.C., Bachmeier, A.S., Schmit, T.J., Partain, P.T. & Noh, Y.-J.** 2013. Earth-viewing satellite perspectives on the Chelyabinsk meteor event. *Proceedings of the National Academy of Sciences,* 110(45): 18092-18097. https://doi.org/10.1073/pnas.1307965110

90 **Lund, S., Manyika, J., Woetzel, J., Barriball, E. & Krishnan, M.** 2020. *Risk, resilience, and rebalancing in global value chains. Mckinsey & Company. https://www.mckinsey.com.*

91 **Range, M., Arbic, B., Johnson, B., Moore, T., Titov, V., Adcroft, A., Ansong, J., Hollis, C., Ritsema, J. & Scotese, C.** 2022. The Chicxulub impact produced a powerful global tsunami. *AGU Advances,* 3(5): e2021AV000627. https://doi.org/10.1029/2021AV000627

92 **Elkamhi, R.** 2008 Three essays on credit risk, fixed income and derivatives. Canada. McGill University.

93 **Lambert, N.M., Fincham, F.D. & Stillman, T.F.** 2012. Gratitude and depressive symptoms: the role of positive reframing and positive emotion. *Cogn Emot,* 26(4): 615-33. https://doi.org/10.1080/02699931.2011.595393

94 **Iglesias, C., Novella, J.M. & Ricci, A.** 2020. *Intelligent environments 2020: Workshop Proceedings of the 16th International Conference on Intelligent Environments.* Vol. 28. IOS Press.

95 **Kimball, B.V.** 2019 Disrupted leadership: strategies and practices of leaders in a VUCA world. CA. Pepperdine University. http://search.proquest.com

96 **Frank, R.** 2013. Covering Captain Cool: The" Miracle on the Hudson" as a Hero Tale. *Western folklore,* 72(1): 59-81. https://www.jstor.org/stable/24550907

97 **Hackmann, H. & Moser, S.** 2013. Social and environmental change in a complex, uncertain world: Introduction to Part 1. In: *World social science report, 2013: changing global environments,* pp. 67-70. UNESCO Digital Library.

98 **Ta, C., Goodchild, A.V. & Ivanov, B.** 2010. Building resilience into freight transportation systems. *Transportation Research Record: Journal of the Transportation Research Board,* 2168(1): 129-135. https://doi.org/10.3141/2168-15

99 **Mamo, L.T.** 2020. Insights from Africa's Covid-19 response: repurposing manufacturing. *Tony Blair Institute for Global Change, London.*

100 **Pandey, R., Massand, A., Mulya, V.T., Sin, L.G., Naresh, V.P., Zamara, F.B., Kee, D.M.H., Zamri, S.K.B., Azmi, N.A.S.B. & Hamdan, N.N.B.M.** 2021. The Impacts of Covid-19 on Unilever. *Journal of the Community Development in Asia (JCDA),* 4(1): 34-43. https://doi.org/10.32535/jcda.v4i1.996

101 **Xie, J. & Youn, C.** 2020. How the luxury fashion brand adjust to deal with the COVID-19. *International Journal of Costume and Fashion,* 20(2): 50-60. https://ijcf.ksc.or.kr/xml/27495/27495.pdf

102 **Grant, J. & Wunder, T.** 2021. Strategic transformation to sustilience: learning from COVID-19. *Journal of Strategy*

and Management, 14(3): 331-351. https://doi.org/10.1108/JSMA-07-2021-0151

103 **Gweh, G.N. & Bekana, D.M.** 2021. Organizational risk management practices in time of crisis: An exploratory case study of Ethiopian Airlines in the Corona Virus pandemic. *Journal of Business and Administrative Studies,* 13(2): 1-37. https://doi.org/10.20372/jbas.v13i2.4456

104 **Raetze, S.** 2020. *What makes work teams resilient? An overview of resilience processes and cross-level antecedents.* Research Handbook on Organizational Resilience. Edward Elgar Publishing.

105 **Johansson, C. & Bäck, E.** 2017. Strategic leadership communication for crisis network coordination. *International Journal of Strategic Communication,* 11(4): 324-343. https://doi.org/10.1080/1553118x.2017.1341889

106 **Alam, N.** 2022. Fintech regulation - a key to financial stability. In: *Global Perspectives in FinTech: Law, Finance and Technology,* pp. 9-24. Springer.

107 **Ahmed, E., Kilika, J. & Gakenia, C.** 2021. SME Resilience to Covid-19. *International Journal of Finance & Banking Studies (2147-4486),* 10(4): 24-39. https://doi.org/10.20525/ijfbs.v10i4.1399

108 **Kruger, J.-P.** 2017 A strategic thinking approach to the delivery of a creative and adaptive strategy. South Africa. University of Pretoria. Unpublished Doctorate Dissertation. https://repository.up.ac.za/handle/2263/65490

109 **Patriarca, R., Di Gravio, G., Costantino, F., Falegnami, A. & Bilotta, F.** 2018. An analytic framework to assess organizational resilience. *Saf Health Work,* 9(3): 265-276. https://doi.org/10.10.16/j.shaw.2017.10.005

110 **Robbins, D.K. & Pearce, J.A.** 1992. Turnaround: Recovery and retrenchment. *Strategic management journal,* 13(4): 287-309. https://doi.org/10.1002/smj.4250130404

111 **Whitley, R.** 2008. *Constructing universities as strategic actors: limitations and variations. In The University in the Market (pp. 23-37). (Wenner-Gren International Series; Vol. 84).*

Portland Press Ltd. https://research.manchester.ac.uk/en/publications/constructing-universities-as-strategic-actors-limitations-and-var

112 **Ryan, E.V. & Ryan, W.H.** 2013. Ground-based Near-Earth Object studies in the post-Russian (Chelyabinsk) meteor airburst world. Conference presentation at Ground-based Near-Earth Object studies in the post-Russian (Chelyabinsk) meteor airburst world. Proceedings of the Advanced Maui Optical and Space Surveillance Technologies Conference, held in Wailea, Maui, Hawaii, September 10-13, 2013, Ed.: S. Ryan, The Maui Economic Development Board, id.E101. https://commons.erau.edu/publication/58/

113 **Zawawi, N.M., Abd Wahab, S., Al-Mamun, A., Yaacob, A.S., Samy, N.K.A. & Fazal, S.A.** 2016. Defining the concept of innovation and firm innovativeness: a critical analysis from resorce-based view perspective. *International Journal of Business and Management,* 11(6): 1-87. https://doi.org/10.5539/ijbm.v11n6p87

114 **Nasierowski, W. & Arcelus, F.J.** 2012. What is innovativeness: literature review. *foundations of management,* 4(1): 63-74. https://doi.org/10.2478/fman-2013-0004

115 **Golgeci, I. & Y. Ponomarov, S.** 2013. Does firm innovativeness enable effective responses to supply chain disruptions? An empirical study. *Supply Chain Management: An International Journal,* 18(6): 604-617. https://doi.org/10.1108/SCM-10-2012-0331

116 **Cefis, E. & Marsili, O.** 2003. Survivor: the role of innovation in firm's survival. *Journal of Business Research,* 61(7): 753-764. https://doi.org/10.1016/j.respol.2006.02.006

117 **Centobelli, P., Cerchione, R. & Ertz, M.** 2020. Agile supply chain management: where did it come from and where will it go in the era of digital transformation? *Industrial Marketing Management,* 90: 324-345. https://doi.org/10.1016/j.indmarman.2020.07.011

118 **Brosseau, D., Ebrahim, S., Handscomb, C. & Thaker, S.** 2019. The journey to an agile organization. *McKinsey &*

Company, May,* 10: 14-27. https://www.mckinsey.com/capabilities/people-and-organizational-performance/our-insights/the-journey-to-an-agile-organization

119 **Fitriasari, F.** 2020. How do small and medium enterprise (SME) survive the COVID-19 outbreak? *Jurnal Inovasi Ekonomi,* 5(02). https://doi.org/10.22219/jiko.v5i3.11838

120 **Emmanuel-Yusuf, D.** 2018 Resilience in supply chains: An analytical framework for the UK wood fuel sector. UK. University of Surrey. Unpublished Doctorate Dissertation. https://openresearch.surrey.ac.uk/esploro/outputs/doctoral/Resilience-in-supply-chains-RELISC-an/99512093902346

121 **Campos, K.** 2016. Dimensions of business resilience in the context of post-disaster recovery in Davao City, Philippines. *Review of Integrative Business & Economics Research,* 5(1): 168-198. Available at SSRN: https://ssrn.com/abstract=2862400

122 **Wardman, J.K.** 2020. Recalibrating pandemic risk leadership: Thirteen crisis ready strategies for COVID-19. *Journal of Risk Research,* 23(7-8): 1092-1120. https://doi.org/10.1080/13669877.2020.1842989

123 **Palmi, P., Morrone, D., Miglietta, P.P. & Fusco, G.** 2018. How did organizational resilience work before and after the financial crisis? An empirical study. *International Journal of Business and Management,* 13(10): 54-62. https://doi.org/0.5539/ijbm.v13n10p54

124 **Dalton, T. & Kim, J.** 2023. Rethinking arms control with a nuclear North Korea. *Survival,* 65(1): 21-48. https://carnegieendowment.org/publications/88980

125 **Upadhyaya, D.** 1965. *Integral humanism.* Bharatiya Janta Party. https://www.bjp.org/integralhumanism.

126 **Zhongming, Z., Linong, L., Xiaona, Y., Wangqiang, Z. & Wei, L.** 2019. High-speed videos capture how kangaroo rat escapes rattlesnake attack. Retrieved from: https://www.sci.news/biology/ninja-kangaroo-rats-07085.html

127 **Miles, D.C., Burrus, K.R. & Shoemaker, K.T.** 2020. First records of california kangaroo rats, dipodomys californicus, in nevada. *Northwestern Naturalist,* 101(1): 61-63. https://doi.org/10.1898/1051-1733-101.1.61

128 **Liu, Y. & Ben-Tzvi, P.** 2022. *How a serpentine tail assists agile motions of kangaroo rats: a dynamics and control approach.* https://doi.org/10.21203/rs.3.rs-1315822/v1

129 **Karacay, M.** 2017 Slack-performance relationship before, during and after a financial crisis: empirical evidence from European manufacturing firms. UK. University of Birmingham. Unpublished Doctorate Dissertation.

130 **Omar, A.R.C., Ishak, S. & Jusoh, M.A.** 2020. The impact of Covid-19 movement control order on SMEs' businesses and survival strategies. *Geografia,* 16(2). https://doi.org/10.17576/geo-2020-1602-11

131 **Gupta, R. & Sebastian, V.J.** 2017. Configuration approach to strategic & entrepreneurial orientation construct & amp; small firm growth: Evidence from India. *Theoretical Economics Letters,* 07(05): 1261-1281. https://doi.org/10.4236/tel.2017.75086

132 **Che Omar, A.R., Ishak, S. & Jusoh, M.A.** 2020. The impact of Covid-19 Movement Control Order on SMEs' businesses and survival strategies. *Malaysian Journal of Society and Space,* 16(2): 139-150. https://doi.org/10.17576/geo-2020-1602-11

133 **Vanacker, T., Collewaert, V. & Zahra, S.A.** 2016. Slack resources, firm performance, and the institutional context: Evidence from privately heldEuropean firms. *Strategic management journal,* 38(6): 1305-1326. https://doi.org/10.1002/smj.2583

134 **Stellian, R. & Danna-Buitrago, J.P.** 2019. Financial distress, free cash flow, and interfirm payment network: Evidence from an agent-based model. *International Journal of Finance & Economics,* 25(4): 598-616. https://doi.org/10.1002/ijfe.1769

135 **Hailu, D.H., Wang, M., Ibrahim, A.A. & Ayalew, M.M.** 2020. Financial slack and firm performance: Evidence from Africa. *Global Journal of Management And Business Research,* 2(4). https://journalofbusiness.org/index.php/GJMBR/article/view/3232

136 **Townsley, M. & DeColfmacker, R.** 2021. *Cash defines survival: Cash is king.* Gatekeeper Press.

137 **Drehmann, M., Farag, M., Tarashev, N. & Tsatsaronis, K.** 2020. *Buffering Covid-19 losses-the role of prudential policy.* Retrieved from: https://www.bis.org/publ/bisbull09.pdf

138 **Carletti, E., Claessens, S., Fatás, A. & Vives, X.** 2020. *Barcelona report 2-the bank business model in the post-Covid-19 world.* Centre for Economic Policy Research.

139 **Wieczorek-Kosmala, M.** 2021. COVID-19 impact on the hospitality industry: Exploratory study of financial-slack-driven risk preparedness. *Int J Hosp Manag,* 94: 102799. https://doi.org/10.1016/j.ijhm.2020.102799

140 **Bialowolski, P., Weziak-Bialowolska, D., Lee, M.T., Chen, Y., VanderWeele, T.J. & McNeely, E.** 2021. The role of financial conditions for physical and mental health. Evidence from a longitudinal survey and insurance claims data. *Soc Sci Med,* 281: 114041. https://doi.org/10.1016/j.socscimed.2021.114041

141 **Mbogo, F.** 2013 Challenges of internationalization experienced by Barclays Bank of Kenya. Nairobi. University of Nairobi. MBA. http://erepository.uonbi.ac.ke/handle/11295/58545

142 **Nguyen, P.V., Huynh, H.T.N., Trieu, H.D.X. & Tran, K.T.** 2019. Internationalization, strategic slack resources, and firm performance: The case study of Vietnamese enterprises. *Journal of Risk and Financial Management,* 12(3): 1-24. https://doi.org/10.3390/jrfm12030144

143 **Rafailov, D.** 2017. Financial slack and performance of Bulgarian firms. *Journal of Finance and Bank Management,* 5(2): 1-13. https://doi.org/10.15640/jfbm.v5n2a1

144 **Bosshardt, J. & Kakhbod, A.** 2021. Why did firms draw down their credit lines during the covid-19 shutdown? *SSRN Electronic Journal.* https://doi.org/10.2139/ssrn.3696981

145 **Goel, T. & Garralda, J.M.S.** 2020. *Bonds and syndicated loans during the Covid-19 crisis: decoupled again?*

146 **Garthwaite, C., Busse, M., Brown, J. & Merkley, G.** 2017. Starbucks: A story of growth. *Kellogg School of Management Cases,* 5-211-259 https://www.kellogg.northwestern.edu/faculty/research/researchdetail?guid=2d22dba3-bf95-481c-ba92-a62148a61897

147 **O'Neal, L.** 2021. Save Our Community Stages: How Providing Federal Relief to Community Theaters during COVID-19 Can Benefit All Nonprofits. *Loy. J. Pub. Int. L.,* 23: 44.

148 **Klewes, J. & Wreschniok, R.** 2009. Reputation capital Building and maintaining trust in the 21st century. In: *Reputation Capital: Building and Maintaining Trust in the 21st Century,* pp. 1-8. Springer.

149 **Schultz, M.C. & Schultz, J.T.** 1990. Corporate Strategy in Crisis Management: Johnson & Johnson and Tylenol. *Essays in Economic and Business History,* 7(A): 164. https://doi.org/https://commons.erau.edu/publication/58/

150 **Rushe, D.** 2013. Deepwater oil spill a classic failure of BP management, court hears. *The Guardian,* 26: 2013. https://www.theguardian.com/environment/2013/feb/26/deepwater-oil-spill-trial-bp-failure

151 **Tracey, N. & French, E.** 2017. Influence your firm's resilience through its reputation: results won't happen overnight but they will happen! *Corporate Reputation Review,* 20(1): 57-75. https://doi.org/10.1057/s41299-017-0014-7

152 **Jackson, K.T.** 2004. *Building reputational capital: Strategies for integrity and fair play that improve the bottom line.* Oxford University Press.

153 **Coulibaly, B., Sapriza, H. & Zlate, A.** 2011. *Trade credit and international trade during the 2008-09 global financial crisis.* Board of Governors of the Federal Reserve System Washington, DC.

154 **Šontaitė-Petkevičienė, M.** 2014. Crisis management to avoid damage for corporate reputation: the case of retail chain crisis in the Baltic countries. *Procedia-Social and Behavioral Sciences,* 156: 452-457. https://doi.org/10.1016/j.sbspro.2014.11.220

155 **Gao, C., Zuzul, T., Jones, G. & Khanna, T.** 2017. Overcoming institutional voids: A reputation-based view of long-run survival. Institution.

156 **Dubey, R., Altay, N., Gunasekaran, A., Blome, C., Papadopoulos, T. & Childe, S.J.** 2018. Supply chain agility, adaptability and alignment. *International Journal of Operations*

& Production Management, 38(1): 129-148. https://doi.org/10.1108/ijopm-04-2016-0173

157 **Al-afifi, A.** 2015 Leadership best practice for sustaining business excellence in innovative organisations. United Kingdom. Sheffield Hallam University. Unpublished Doctorate Dissertation. http://shura.shu.ac.uk/19229/

158 **Masood, O., Aktan, B., Turen, S., Javaria, K. & Sayed Abou ElSeoud, M.** 2017. Which resources matter the most to firm performance? An experimental study on Malaysian listed firms. *Problems and perspectives in management,* 15(2): 74-80. https://doi.org/10.21511/ppm.15(2).2017.07

159 **Cameron-Blake, E., Breton, C., Sim, P., Tatlow, H., Hale, T., Wood, A., Smith, J., Sawatsky, J., Parsons, Z. & Tyson, K.** 2021. Variation in the Canadian provincial and territorial responses to COVID-19. *Blavatnik School of Government Working Paper Series,* 39. www.bsg.ox.ac.uk/covidtracker

160 **Waddock, S.** 2000. The multiple bottom lines of corporate citizenship: Social investing, reputation, and responsibility audits. *Business and Society Review,* 105(3): 323-345. https://doi.org/10.1111/0045-3609.00085

161 **Kungu, G., Desta, I. & Ngui, T.** 2014. An assessment of the effectiveness of competitive strategies by commercial banks: A Case of Equity Bank. *International Journal of Education and Research,* 2(12): 333-346. https://www.semanticscholar.org/paper/An-Assessment-of-the-Effectiveness-of-Competitive-A-Kungu-Desta/3dc791e190b5c3071c3d19ef61d6aecf1e0e6b71

162 **Kiganda, E.O.** 2014. Effect of macroeconomic factors on commercial banks profitability in Kenya: Case of equity bank limited. *Journal of Economics and Sustainable development,* 5(2): 46-56. https://www.iiste.org/Journals/index.php/JEDS/article/view/10697

163 **Gallaugher, J. & Ransbotham, S.** 2010. Social media and customer dialog management at Starbucks. *MIS Quarterly Executive,* 9(4): 1-17. https://hospitalityandtravel.files.wordpress.com/2012/10/social-media-and-customer-dialog.pdf

164 **Kohnen, J.** 2012. Onward: How Starbucks fought for its life without losing its soul. *The Quality Management Journal,* 19(2): 64. https://doi.org/10.1080/10686967.2012.11918349

165 **Avila, M., Parkin, H. & Galoostian, S.** 2019. $16.7 million to save one reputation: How Starbucks responded amidst a racial sensitivity crisis. *Pepperdine Journal of Communication Research,* 7(1): 4. https://digitalcommons.pepperdine.edu/pjcr/vol7/iss1/4/

166 **Leka, S. & Houdmont, J.** 2010. *Occupational health psychology.* John Wiley & Sons.

167 **Denyer, D.** 2017. Organizational Resilience: A summary of academic evidence, business insights and new thinking. *BSI and Cranfield School of Management*: 8-25. https://www.cranfield.ac.uk

168 **Crawford, M.H.** 1989. Pacific Balloonists to Sample Jet Stream. *Science,* 246(4934): 1117-1117. https://doi.org/10.1126/science.246.4934.1117-d

169 **Cui, T., Ye, J.H. & Tan, C.H.** 2022. Information technology in open innovation: A resource orchestration perspective. *Information & Management,* 52(3): 348-358. https://doi.org/10.1016/j.im.2014.12.005

170 **Arrighetti, A., Landini, F. & Bartoloni, E.** 2018. *Firm survival during economic downturns: is selecton based on cleansing or skill accumulation? Department of Economics, Parma University (Italy).* https://ideas.repec.org/p/par/dipeco/2018-ep04.html

171 **Dolev, N., Itzkovich, Y. & Katzman, B.** 2021. A gender-focused prism on the long-term impact of teachers' emotional mistreatment on resilience: Do men and women differ in their quest for social-emotional resources in a masculine society? *Sustainability,* 13(17): 1-15. https://doi.org/10.3390/su13179832

172 **Sirmon, D.G., Barney, J.B., Ketchen, D.J., Wright, M., Hitt, M.A., Ireland, R.D. & Gilbert, B.A.** 2010. Resource orchestration to create competitive advantage. *Journal of Management,* 37(5): 1390-1412. https://doi.org/10.1177/0149206310385695

173 **Dubrovski, D.** 2020. Developmental and technological restructuring for the implementation of competitive business

models. *Management,* 20: 22. https://ideas.repec.org/h/tkp/mklp20/279-288.html

174 **Hitt, M.A., Arregle, J.L. & Holmes, R.M.** 2020. Strategic management theory in a post-pandemic and non-ergodic world. *Journal of management studies,* 58(1): 259-264. https://doi.org/10.1111/joms

175 **Carnes, C.M., Chirico, F., Hitt, M.A., Huh, D.W. & Pisano, V.** 2017. Resource Orchestration for Innovation: Structuring and Bundling Resources in Growth- and Maturity-Stage Firms. *Long range planning,* 50(4): 472-486. https://doi.org/10.1016/j.lrp.2016.07.003

176 **Boon, C., Eckardt, R., Lepak, D.P. & Boselie, P.** 2017. Integrating strategic human capital and strategic human resource management. *The International Journal of Human Resource Management,* 29(1): 34-67. https://doi.org/10.1080/09585192.2017.1380063

177 **Tyce, M.** 2020. Beyond the neoliberal-statist divide on the drivers of innovation: A political settlements reading of Kenya's M-Pesa success story. *World Development,* 125: 1-14. https://doi.org/10.1016/j.worlddev.2019.104621

178 **Boss, D.S.** 2014 Capabilities, configurations, and leveraging strategies: An investigation of the leveraging process of resource orchestration. Texas, USA. Texas A&M University. Unpublished Doctorate Dissertation. https://oaktrust.library.tamu.edu/handle/1969.1/153824?show=full

179 **Chen, R., Xie, Y. & Liu, Y.** 2021. Defining, Conceptualizing, and Measuring Organizational Resilience: A Multiple Case Study. *Sustainability,* 13(5): 1-25. https://doi.org/10.3390/su13052517

180 **Peuscher, D.W.** 2016 The resource orchestration theory as contributor to supply chain management: An assessment on its applicability. Netherlands. University of Twente. Unpublished Doctorate Dissertation. https://essay.utwente.nl/70993/

181 **Guha, B.** 2002. Rationalisation of workforce-an integral part of structural adjustment. *Indian Journal of Industrial Relations,* 37(4): 505-527. https://www.jstor.org/stable/27767809

182 **Pearce, J.A. & Robbins, K.** 1993. Toward improved theory and research on business turnaround. *Journal of Management,* 19(3): 613-636. https://doi.org/10.1177/014920639301900306

183 **Tshuma, M.** 2022. Midland State University skewed retrenchment scheme backfires. *CITE.* https://cite.org.zw/msus-skewed-retrenchment-scheme-backfires/

184 **Bassey, B., Edom, G. & Aganyi, A.** 2016. Assessing the impact of retained profit on corporate performance: Empirical evidence from Niger mills company, Calabar-Nigeria. *European Journal of Business and Innovation Research,* 4(1): 36-47. https://www.eajournals.org/

185 **Kess, S. & Mendlowitz, E.** 2016. Using Warren Buffett's rules to assist individual investors. *The CPA Journal,* 86(11): 62-64. https://www.cpajournal.com/2016/11/23/pfp-using-warren-buffetts-rules-assist-individual-investors/

186 **Nandonde, F.** 2021. In the desire of conquering East African supermarket business: What went wrong in Nakumatt supermarket. *Emerging Economies Cases Journal,* 2(1). https://doi.org/10.1177/2516604221999224

187 **Ahuja, S. & Chan, Y.E.** 2017. Resource orchestration for IT-enabled innovation. *Kindai management review,* 5(1): 78-96. https://www.kindai.ac.jp/files/rd/research-center/management-innovation/kindai-management-review/vol5_5.pdf

188 **Agatha, N.** 2022 Effect of innovation and technology as a strategy on customer retention at the Equity Bank Kenya Limited. Nairobi. University of Nairobi. MBA. http://erepository.uonbi.ac.ke/handle/11295/162271

189 **Gachigo, J., Ondigo, H., Aduda, J. & Onsomu, Z.** 2022. Moderating role of institutional characteristics on the relationship between mergers & acquisition strategies and financial performance of commercial banks in Kenya. *African Development Finance Journal,* 1(2): 65-94. http://www.uonjournals.uonbi.ac.ke/ojs/index.php/adfj/article/view/895

190 **Thomas, D.** 2019. After Collymore: Safaricom faces the future. *African Business,* (466): 10-14. https://african.business/2019/09/economy/after-collymore-safaricom-faces-the-future

191　**Servaes, H. & Tamayo, A.** 2017. The role of social capital in corporations: a review. *Oxford Review of Economic Policy,* 33(2): 201-220. https://doi.org/10.1093/oxrep/grx026

192　**Gabbay, S. & Leenders, R.** 2002. Social capital of organizations: From social structure to the management of corporate social capital. *Research in the Sociology of Organizations,* 18. https://doi.org/10.1016/S0733-558X(01)18001-8

193　**Prusak, L. & Cohen, D.** 2001. How to invest in social capital. *Harvard Business Review,* 79(6): 86-97. https://hbr.org/2001/06/how-to-invest-in-social-capital

194　**Berseck, N.** 2018. *Resource orchestration as source of competitive advantage of cities—empirical studies of business improvement districts in New York City and the City of Hamburg.* Technische Universitaet Berlin (Germany).

195　**Franzen, G. & Moriarty, S.** 2008. *The science and art of branding.* ME Sharpe.

196　**Otfinoski, S.** 2019. *Captain Sully's River landing: The Hudson hero of Flight 1549.* Tangled History.

197　**Stiegler, M.P.** 2015. What I learned about adverse events from Captain Sully: It's not what you think. *Jama,* 313(4): 361-362. https://doi.org/doi.org/10.1001/jama.2014.16025

198　**Muthimi, J.K. & Kilika, J.M.** 2018. Leadership strategy, behavioural focus and firm performance: A review of literature. *International Business Research,* 11(11): 143-163. https://doi.org/10.5539/ibr.v11n11p143

199　**Folan, L.N.** 2019 Defining a research model of leader resilience and evaluating the dispositional effect of resilience on transformational leadership. Perth, Australia. Murdoch University. Unpublished Doctorate Dissertation. http://researchrepository.murdoch.edu.au/id/eprint/52183

200　**Ireland, R.D., Hoskisson, R.E. & Hitt, M.A.** 2014. *Strategic management: concepts and cases: competitiveness and globalization.* Vol. 201. Boston: South-Western College Publishing, South-Western Cengage Learning.

201　**Lucas, H.C.** 2012. *The search for survival: Lessons from disruptive technologies.* ABC-CLIO.

202 **Roy, A.** 2012. Relationship of osmosis: Rise of Emirates, The airline and Dubai, the city. *Academy of Taiwan Business Management Review.* Available at: http://hdl.handle.net/10536/DRO/DU:30051311

203 **Chanduví, D.A.G., Lama, G.L.R. & Morey, N.D.** 2015. Analysis of research literature of professional competency models with a cognitive-motivational approach. *Procedia - Social and Behavioral Sciences,* 171: 1400-1409. https://doi.org/10.1016/j.sbspro.2015.01.260

204 **Cote, R.** 2017. Vision of effective leadership. *International Journal of Business Administration,* 8(6): 1-10. https://doi.org/10.5430/ijba.v8n6p1

205 **Kadalie, D.** 2006. *Leader's resource kit: tools and techniques to develop your leadership.* Evangel Publishing House.

206 **Waithira Ng'ang'a, L., Waiganjo, E.W. & Njeru, A.W.** 2017. Influence of strategic direction on organizational performance in tourism government agencies in Kenya. *International Journal of Business and Commerce,* 6(4): 18-36. www.ijbcnet.com

207 **Babu, S. & Chalam, G.** 2016. Impact of organizational mission and vision and their potential on the performance of employees. *International Journal of Engineering and Management Research (IJEMR),* 6(6): 203-206. https://www.studocu.com/

208 **Ledesma, J.** 2014. Conceptual Frameworks and Research Models on Resilience in Leadership. *SAGE Open,* 4(3): 215-264. https://doi.org/10.1177/2158244014545464

209 **Damak, S.** 2018. The strategic purpose of belonging in martin luther king, jr.'s "I Have a Dream" speech: An African American conforming to Americanity. In: M. Guirat, ed. *Politics and Poetics of Belonging* pp. 214-237. Cambridge Scholars Publishing.

210 **Bowen, S.A.** 2018. Mission and vision. *The international encyclopedia of strategic communication*: 1-9. https://doi.org/10.1002/9781119010722.IESC0111

211 **Halama, P.** 2014. Meaning in life and coping: Sense of meaning as a buffer against stress. In: *Meaning in positive and existential psychology,* pp. 239-250.

212 **Leuthesser, L. & Kohli, C.** 1997. Corporate identity: The role of mission statements. *Business Horizons,* 40(3): 59-66. https://doi.org/10.1016/S0007-6813(97)90053-7

213 **Lampinen, J.** 2020 The true test of leadership is how you lead in times of crisis: Understanding crises in organizations. Finland. Lab University of Applied Sciences. MBA. https://urn.fi/URN:NBN:fi:amk-2020052614041

214 **Southwick, F.S., Martini, B.L., Charney, D.S. & Southwick, S.M.** 2017. Leadership and resilience. In: *Leadership Today,* pp. 315-333. Springer.

215 **Bowers, M.R., Hall, J.R. & Srinivasan, M.M.** 2017. Organizational culture and leadership style: The missing combination for selecting the right leader for effective crisis management. *Business Horizons,* 60(4): 551-563. https://doi.org/10.1016/j.bushor.2017.04.001

216 **Al-Balushi, M.I.A.** 2019 Organizational resilience through quality management: a study on the impact of the implementation of quality management principles on resourcefulness. UK. University of Edinburgh. Unpublished Doctorate Dissertation. https://hdl.handle.net/1842/36841

217 **Johannessen, J. & Stokvik, H.** 2019. 10 strategies for thinking creatively', evidence-based innovation leadership. *Evidence-Based Innovation Leadership*: 173–196. https://doi.org/10.1108/978-1-78769-635-820181011

218 **Johannessen, S.O.** 2018. *Strategies, leadership and complexity in crisis and emergency operations.* NY, Routledge.

219 **Crowley-Henry, M. & Al Ariss, A.** 2016. Talent management of skilled migrants: propositions and an agenda for future research. *The International Journal of Human Resource Management,* 29(13): 2054-2079. https://doi.org/10.1080/09585192.2016.1262889

220 **Pasmore, W., Lafferty, K. & Spencer, S.** 2009. Developing a leadership strategy: A critical ingredient for organizational success. *Greensboro: Center for Creative Leadership.* https://www.ccl.org/wp-content/uploads/2015/04/DevelopingLeadershipStrategy.pdf

221 **Siddiqui, A.T.** 2017. Can employee training and development increase organizational resilience against economic crises? *International Journal of Managerial Studies and Research*, 5(4): 78-82. https://doi.org/10.20431/2349-0349.0504011

222 **Mahmoud, A.B., Fuxman, L., Mohr, I., Reisel, W.D. & Grigoriou, N.** 2021. "We aren't your reincarnation!" workplace motivation across X, Y and Z generations. *International Journal of Manpower*, 42(1): 193-209. https://doi.org/10.1108/IJM-09-2019-0448

223 **Seibert, M.** 2018. Systems thinking and how it can help build a sustainable world: A beginning conversation. *The Solutions Journal*, 9(3): 1-9. https://mahb.stanford.edu/wp-content/uploads/2018/11/MAHBBonusBlog_SystemsThinkingandSustainability_Seibert-2018.pdf

224 **Benitez, M.A., Velasco, C., Sequeira, A.R., Henriquez, J., Menezes, F.M. & Paolucci, F.** 2020. Responses to COVID-19 in five Latin American countries. *Health Policy Technol*, 9(4): 525-559. https://doi.org/10.1016/j.hlpt.2020.08.014

225 **John, M.** 2019. Venezuelan economic crisis: crossing Latin American and Caribbean borders. *Migration and Development*, 8(3): 437-447. https://doi.org/10.1080/21632324.2018.1502003

226 **Stoverink, A.C., Kirkman, B.L., Mistry, S. & Rosen, B.** 2020. Bouncing back together: Toward a theoretical model of work team resilience. *Academy of Management Review*, 45(2): 395-422. https://doi.org/10.5465/amr.2017.0005

227 **Turgeon, P.E.** 2019 Identifying the leadership skills needed to develop the competencies to lead in a postcrisis organization: A delphi study. USA. Brandman University. Unpublished Doctorate Dissertation. https://digitalcommons.umassglobal.edu/cgi/viewcontent.cgi?article=1305&context=edd_dissertations

228 **Benzidia, S., Luca, R.M. & Boiko, S.** 2021. Disruptive innovation, business models, and encroachment strategies: Buyer's perspective on electric and hybrid vehicle technology. *Technological Forecasting and Social Change*, 165(C). https://doi.org/10.1016/j.techfore.2020.120520

229 **Razzouk, R. & Shute, V.** 2012. What is design thinking and why is it important? *Review of educational research,* 82(3): 330-348. https://doi.org/10.3102/0034654312457429

230 **Downes, L. & Nunes, P.F.** 2014. *Big-bang disruption.* Harvard Business Review Press.

231 **Fener, T. & Cevik, T.** 2015. Leadership in crisis management: Separation of leadership and executive concepts. *Procedia Economics and Finance,* 26: 695-701. https://doi.org/1016/S2212-5671(15)00817-5

232 **Vaughn, G.J., Sugerman, K.S. & Furman, M.I.** 2020. The power and importance of leadership in a crisis. *New England Journal of Medicine,* 1(4). https://doi.org/10.1056/CAT.20.0314

233 **Stilwell, R.A. & Pasmore, W.** 2016. Change leader behavior inventory: Development and validation of an assessment instrument. *The Journal of Applied Behavioral Science,* 52(4): 373-395. https://doi.org/10.1177/0021886316663406

234 **Spieser, J.-M.** 1998. The representation of Christ in the apses of early Christian churches. *Gesta,* 37(1): 63-73. https://doi.org/10.2307/767213

235 **Shivaranjani, G.** 2018 Adversity quotient profiling for women employees of commercial banks. India. Anna University. Unpublished Doctorate Dissertation.

236 **Mannucci, P.V., Orazi, D.C. & de Valck, K.** 2021. Developing improvisation skills: The influence of individual orientations. *Administrative Science Quarterly,* 66(3): 612-658. https://doi.org/10.1177/0001839220975697

237 **Ariratana, W., Sirisookslip, S. & Ngang, T.K.** 2015. Development of leadership soft skills among educational administrators. *Procedia - Social and Behavioral Sciences,* 186: 331-336. https://doi.org/10.1016/j.sbspro.2015.04.016

238 **Ulfig, Y.M.** 2019 Leadership strategies for increasing employee engagement in the service industry. MN. Walden University. https://scholarworks.waldenu.edu/dissertations/6694/

239 **Regester, M. & Larkin, J.** 2008. *Risk issues and crisis management in public relations: A casebook of best practice.* Kogan Page Publishers.

240 **McDevitt, M.A., Cobble, W.E., Gaffney, H. & Gause, K.E.** 2004. *The changing nature of warfare.* https://apps.dtic.mil/sti/pdfs/AD1014537.pdf

241 **Harrysson, M., Metayer, E. & Sarrazin, H.** 2012. How 'social intelligence'can guide decisions. *McKinsey Quarterly,* 4(1): 81-89. https://www.mckinsey.com/industries/technology-media-and-telecommunications/our-insights/how-social-intelligence-can-guide-decisions

242 **Brown, F.W. & Moshavi, D.** 2005. Transformational leadership and emotional intelligence: A potential pathway for an increased understanding of interpersonal influence. *Journal of Organizational Behavior: The International Journal of Industrial, Occupational and Organizational Psychology and Behavior,* 26(7): 867-871. https://doi.org/10.1002/job.334

243 **Armstrong, A.R., Galligan, R.F. & Critchley, C.R.** 2011. Emotional intelligence and psychological resilience to negative life events. *Personality and Individual Differences,* 51(3): 331-336. https://doi.org/10.1016/j.paid.2011.03.025

244 **Aggarwal, A.** 2021. *Global framework on core skills for life and work in the 21st century. International Labor Organisation.* https://www.ilo.org

245 **Orejarena, H., Zambrano, O. & Carvajal, M.** 2019. Emotional intelligence and its influence on organizational leadership in the VUCA world. Conference presentation at 4th International Conference on Social, Business, and Academic Leadership (ICSBAL 2019). Atlantis Press. https://doi.org/10.2991/icsbal-19.2019.32

246 **Schwartz, M.L.** 2013 Emotional intelligence in hypercrisis: A content analysis of World Trade Center leadership response to the terrorist attacks of September 11, 2001. USA. Wright State University. Master of Science. https://corescholar.libraries.wright.edu/etd_all/710/

247 **Puchalski, C.M., Vitillo, R., Hull, S.K. & Reller, N.** 2014. Improving the spiritual dimension of whole person care: reaching national and international consensus. *J Palliat Med,* 17(6): 642-56. https://doi.org/10.1089/jpm.2014.9427

248 **Sahebalzamani, M., Farahani, H., Abasi, R. & Talebi, M.** 2013. The relationship between spiritual intelligence with psychological well-being and purpose in life of nurses. *Iranian journal of nursing and midwifery research,* 18(1): 38-41. https://pubmed.ncbi.nlm.nih.gov/23983726/

249 **Shaari, S. & Matore, M.E.E.M.** 2019. Emphasizing the concept of spiritual intelligence from Islamic and Western perspectives on multiple intelligence. *Creative Education,* 10(12): 2815-2830. https://doi.org/10.4236/ce.2019.1012208

250 **Emecheta Bartholomew, C. & Hart, A.** 2019. Spiritual capital and organisational resilience of banks in Anambra state South-Eastern State of Nigeria. *World Journal of Innovative Research,* 6(2): 109- 125. www.wjir.org

251 **Petrus, M.V., Siti, A.E., Kusdi, R. & Andriani, K.** 2018. The influence of spiritual intelligence on job stress and turnover intention. *Russian Journal of Agricultural and Socio-Economic Sciences,* 83(11): 247-253. https://doi.org/10.18551/rjoas.2018-11.29

252 **Northouse, P.G.** 2016. *Leadership theory and practice.* CA, Sage Publications.

253 **Robinson, S. & Judge, T.** 2013. *Organizational behavior.* NJ, Prentice Hall.

254 **Kotter, J.P.** 2012. *Leading change.* Harvard business press.

255 **Ruffman, A.** 1999. *Titanic remembered: The unsinkable ship and Halifax.* Formac Publishing Company.

256 **Cole, M.D.** 2013. *Unsinkable!: The Titanic Shipwreck.* Enslow Publishing, LLC.

257 **Marshall, L.** 1998. *Sinking of the Titanic and great sea disasters a detailed and accurate account.* The Vision Forum.

258 **Lord, W.** 2012. *The night lives on: The untold stories and secrets behind the sinking of the" unsinkable" ship—Titanic.* Open Road Media.

259 **Frey, B., Savage, D. & Torgler, B.** 2009. Surviving the Titanic disaster: economic, natural and social determinants. *SSRN Electronic Journal.* https://doi.org/10.2139/ssrn.1347962

260 **Yu, F.-L.T.** 2012. The sinking of the unsinkable Titanic: Mental inertia and coordination failures. *Human Systems Management,* 31(4): 177-186. https://doi.org/10.3233/HSM-2012-0766

261 **Moosa, I.** 2010. The myth of too big to fail. *Journal of banking regulation,* 11: 319-333. https://doi.org/10.1057/jbr.2010.15

262 **Appiah, K.O., Chizema, A. & Arthur, J.** 2015. Predicting corporate failure: a systematic literature review of methodological issues. *International Journal of Law and Management,* 57(5): 461-485. https://doi.org/10.1108/IJLMA-04-2014-0032

263 **Veganzones, D. & Severin, E.** 2021. Corporate failure prediction models in the twenty-first century: a review. *European Business Review,* 33(2): 204-226. https://doi.org/10.1108/EBR-12-2018-0209

264 **Maxwell, J.** n.d. Everything rises and falls on leadership. BrainyQuote.com. Retrieved April 28, 2023, from https://www.brainyquote.com/quotes/john_c_maxwell_600859.

265 **Akhigbe, A., Martin, A. & Whyte, A.-M.** 2005. Contagion effects of the world's largest bankruptcy: The case of WorldCom. *The Quarterly Review of Economics and Finance,* 45(1): 48-64. https://doi.org/10.1016/j.qref.2004.07.002

266 **Weld, L.G., Bergevin, P.M. & Magrath, L.** 2004. Anatomy of a financial fraud: A forensic examination of healthsouth. *The CPA Journal,* 74(10): 44-60. http://archives.cpajournal.com/2004/1004/essentials/p44.htm

267 **Kemmerer, C.H. & Shawver, T.J.** 2007. Tyco: A top-down approach to ethical failure. *Available at SSRN 1010558.* https://doi.org/10.2139/ssrn.1010558

268 **Miah, M.D. & Haque, A.K.** 2013. Systemic weaknesses of Japanese relationship capitalism: evidence from the case of Livedoor. *World Journal of Social Sciences,* 3(4): 195-211. https://www.sciedupress.com/journal/index.php/wjss/index

269 **Ho, J.C. & Chen, H.** 2018. Managing the disruptive and sustaining the disrupted: The case of Kodak and Fujifilm in the face of digital disruption. *Review of Policy Research,* 35(3): 352-371. https://doi.org/10.1111/ropr.12278

270 **Sutton, R.I., Eisenhardt, K.M. & Jucker, J.V.** 1986. Managing organizational decline: Lessons from Atari. *Organizational dynamics,* 14(4): 17-29. https://doi.org/10.1016/0090-2616(86)90041-0

271 **Fleming, M.J. & Sarkar, A.** 2014. The failure resolution of Lehman Brothers. *Federal Reserve Bank of New York Economic Policy Review,* 20(2). https://www.newyorkfed.org/research/epr/2014/1412flem.html

272 **Baranoff, E.G.** 2011. An analysis of the aig case-understanding systemic risk and its relation to insurance. *Available at SSRN: https://ssrn.com/abstract=1899047.* https://doi.org/10.2139/ssrn.1899047

273 **Suleiman, B.** 2014. The political economy of privatization in Nigeria: A case study of the Nigerian Telecommunications Limited (NITEL). *Research Journal of Sociology,* 2(11): 2-11. https://researchjournali.com/view.php?id=1095

274 **Simo, A.Y.** 2017 Corporate governance: the case of Banco Espírito Santo. Iscte - Instituto Universitário de Lisboa]. Repositório do Iscte. http://hdl.handle.net/10071/16265.

275 **Kim, D.-J.** 2007. Falls from grace and lessons from failure: Daewoo and Medison. *Long range planning,* 40(4-5): 446-464. https://doi.org/10.1016/j.lrp.2007.06.003

276 **Lee, D.G.** 2003. The restructuring of Daewoo. *Economic Crisis and Corporate Restructuring in Korea: Reforming the Chaebol:* 150-180. https://doi.org/10.1017/CBO9781139085083.009

277 **Miller, R.** 2023. Explaining the downfall of BlackBerry in the smartphone market: The role of leadership. *Osaka Jogakuin Junior College,* 19(52): 173-181. http://hdl.handle.net/10775/3808

278 **Ahmed, E.M.A.** 2021. Leadership and organizational distress: Review of literature. *International Journal of Research in Business and Social Science (2147-4478),* 10(6): 1-18. https://doi.org/10.20525/ijrbs.v10i6.1373

279 **Hooper, W. & Rawls, M.K.** 2014. *Borders Group, Inc.'s Final Chapter: How A Bookstore Giant Failed In The Digital Age. Chapter 11 Bankruptcy Case Studies (38).* https://ir.law.utk.edu/utk_studlawbankruptcy/38

280 **Wang, P. & Johnson, C.** 2018. Cybersecurity incident handling: A case study of the equifax data breach *Issues in Information Systems,* 19(3): 150-159. https://iacis.org/iis/2018/3_iis_2018_150-159.pdf

281 **MacKenzie, C.A., Santos, J.R. & Barker, K.** 2012. Measuring changes in international production from a disruption: Case study of the Japanese earthquake and tsunami. *International Journal of Production Economics,* 138(2): 293-302. https://doi.org/10.1016/j.ijpe.2012.03.032

282 **Corey, C.M. & Deitch, E.A.** 2011. Factors affecting business recovery immediately after Hurricane Katrina. *Journal of Contingencies and Crisis management,* 19(3): 169-181. https://doi.org/10.1111/j.1468-5973.2011.00642.x

283 **Smith, R. & Hawkins, B.** 2004. *Lean maintenance: reduce costs, improve quality, and increase market share.* Elsevier.

284 **Garcia Marrero, A.** 2019. The rise of Apple, inc.: Opportunities and challenges in the international marketplace. *Journal for Global Business and Community,* 9(1). https://jgbc.fiu.edu/index.php/Home/article/download/157/155

285 **Helper, S. & Henderson, R.** 2014. Management practices, relational contracts, and the decline of General Motors. *Journal of Economic Perspectives,* 28(1): 49-72. https://doi.org/10.1257/jep.28.1.49

286 **More, R.** 2009. How General Motors lost its focus—and its way. *Ivey Business Journal,* (May-June): 1-16. https://ivey-businessjournal.com/publication/how-general-motors-lost-its-focus-and-its-way/

287 **Senter Jr, R. & McManus, W.** 2013. General motors'road to recovery. *Michigan Sociological Review,* 27(2013): 1-24. https://www.jstor.org/stable/43150986

288 **Khan, M.A. & Hashim, M.** 2014. Organizational change: Case study of General Motors. Conference presentation at ASEE 2014 Zone I Conference, April.

289 **Kumra, G.** 2007. Leading change: An interview with the managing director of Tata Motors. McKinsey Quarterly. https://www.mckinsey.com/capabilities/people-and-organizational

-performance/our-insights/leading-change-an-interview-wit
h-the-managing-director-of-tata-motors

290 **Balbahaith, A.** 2018. Business process improvement in ADNOC gas processing through lean kaizen approach. Conference presentation at Abu Dhabi International Petroleum Exhibition & Conference. Abu Dhabi. https://onepetro.org. https://doi.org/10.2118/193130-MS

291 **D'Agostino, J.L.** 2018 Amazon, E-Commerce, and the New Brand World. University of Oregon. Unpublished Doctorate Dissertation. http://hdl.handle.net/1794/23999

292 **Wada, K.** 2015. Why did Toyota respond less quickly to globalisation? *Entreprises et histoire,* 80(3): 134-154. https://doi.org/10.3917/eh.080.0134

293 **Lee, S.-J.** 2011. Dynamic capabilities at Samsung electronics: analysis of its growth strategy in semiconductors. *Available at SSRN 1914116.* https://doi.org/10.2139/ssrn.1914116

294 **Melnik, J.** 2019. China's "National Champions" Alibaba, Tencent, and Huawei. *Education About Asia,* 24(2): 28-33. https://doi.org/https://www.asianstudies.org/publications/eaa/archives/chinas-national-champions-alibaba-tencent-and-huawei/

295 **Begg, C., Begg, K., Do, E., du Toit, J. & Mills, M.** 2022. Interactions between honey badgers and other predators in the southern Kalahari: Intraguild predation and facilitation. In: *Small carnivores: Evolution, ecology, behaviour, and conservation,* pp. 323-346. Wiley–Blackwel.

296 **Zutshi, A., Mendy, J., Sharma, G.D., Thomas, A. & Sarker, T.** 2021. From challenges to creativity: Enhancing SMEs' resilience in the context of COVID-19. *Sustainability,* 13(12): 6542. https://doi.org/10.3390/su13126542

297 **Nicolescu, O.** 2009. Main features of SMEs organisation system. *Revista de Management Comparat Internaţional,* 10(3): 405-413. https://www.rmci.ase.ro/no10vol3/Vol10_No3_Article1.pdf

298 **Zafar, A. & Mustafa, S.** 2017. SMEs and its role in economic and socio-economic development of Pakistan. *International*

Journal of Academic Research in Accounting, Finance and Management Sciences, 7(4): 195-205. https://doi.org/10.6007/ IJARAFMS/v7-i4/3484

299 **Mateo, E.** 2020. Small and medium enterprise-SMEs resilience model based on maturity cycle. pontificia Universidad Católica del Perú, Perú, jorge.vargas@pucp.edu.pe. https:// www.laccei.org

300 **Berisha, G. & Pula, J.S.** 2015. Defining Small and Medium Enterprises: a critical review. *Academic Journal of Business, Administration, Law and Social Sciences,* 1(1): 17-28. https:// iipccl.org/wp-content/uploads/2015/03/Ajbals-17-28.pdf

301 **Masago, M.O., Okombo, M.O., Alice, S., Reuben, K.G., Chaka, B., Godrick, B. & Joshua, O.K.** 2020. Effects of COVID-19 pandemic on small & middle-income economies (SMEs) in developing nations: A case study of Narok town, Kenya. https://doi.org/10.29333/djfm/9301

302 **Yoshino, N. & Taghizadeh Hesary, F.** 2016. *Major challenges facing small and medium-sized enterprises in Asia and solutions for mitigating them. ADB Institute.* Retrieved from: https://www.adb.org

303 **Fadzil, S. & Rashid, M.** 2022. A design framework for SMEs resilience in Malaysia Conference presentation at IOP Conference Series: Earth and Environmental Science. https:// iopscience.iop.org/article/10.1088/1755-1315/1082/1/012006/ meta. IOP Publishing. https://iopscience.iop.org/ article/10.1088/1755-1315/1082/1/012006/meta

304 **Seville, E., Van Opstal, D. & Vargo, J.** 2015. A primer in resiliency: seven principles for managing the unexpected. *Global Business and Organizational Excellence,* 34(3): 6-18. https://doi. org/10.1002/joe.21600

305 **Alberti, F.G., Ferrario, S. & Pizzurno, E.** 2018. Resilience: resources and strategies of SMEs in a new theoretical framework. *International journal of learning and intellectual capital,* 1(1): 165-188. https://doi.org/10.1504/ijlic.2018.10010129

306 **Munene, I.** 2019. Kenyan universities: On the brink of financial insolvency. *International Higher Education,* (97): 25-27. https://doi.org/10.6017/ihe.2019.97.10949

307 **Kimanga, A.W. & Namande, B.** 2021. Awareness and utilization of electronic resources by postgraduate students at Pan Africa Christian University library, Nairobi, Kenya. *Journal of Applied Information Science,* 9(1): 1-7. http://www.publishing-india.com/jais/

308 **Njoroge, M.C.** 2021 Assessment of the Factors That Influence the Development and Implementation of Strategic Plans in Kenya's Higher Education Institutions: A Case of Kenyatta University and Pan Africa Christian University, Kenya.

309 **Bratianu, C.** 2015. *Organizational knowledge dynamics: Managing knowledge creation, acquisition, sharing, and transformation: Managing knowledge creation, acquisition, sharing, and transformation.* IGI Global.

310 **Boivie, S.R.** 2006 Determinants and consequences of board-level human and social capital. USA. The University of Texas at Austin. Unpublished Doctorate Dissertation. http://hdl.handle.net/2152/12998

311 **Choo, C.W. & Bontis, N.** 2002. *The strategic management of intellectual capital and organizational knowledge.* Oxford university press.

312 **Bartkus, V. & Davis, J.** 2010. *Social capital: Reaching out, reaching in.* Edward Elgar Publishing.

313 **Monconduit, C.** 2007. *Identifiable factors which measure the impact of social capital within schools.* Indiana State University.

314 **Lesser, E.L.** 2000. *Knowledge and social capital: Foundations and applications.* Routledge.

315 **Barnard, B.** 2007. To reach a common goal: insight. *Emergency Services SA,* 28(6): 8-15.

316 **Fleming, R.S.** 2021. Small business resilience and customer retention in times of crisis: Lessons from the Covid-19 Pandemic. *Global Journal of Entrepreneurship,* 5(S1): 30-43. https://www.igbr.org

317 **Russell, R., Atchison, M. & Brooks, R.** 2008. Business plan competitions in tertiary institutions: encouraging entrepreneurship education. *Journal of Higher Education Policy and Management,* 30(2): 123-138. https://doi.org/10.1080/13600800801938739

318 **Cohan, P.S.** 2012. *Hungry start-up strategy: Creating new ventures with limited resources and unlimited vision.* Berrett-Koehler Publishers.

319 **Dahlberg, R. & Guay, F.** 2015. Creating resilient SMEs: Is business continuity management the answer? *WIT Transactions on The Built Environment,* 168: 975-984. https://doi.org/10.2495/SD150852

320 **Mueller, K. & Mueller, E.** 2020. Developing and analysing different definitions of operational excellence. *Leadership, Education, Personality: An Interdisciplinary Journal,* 2(2): 75-80. https://doi.org/10.1365/s42681-020-00017-y

321 **Vaishnavi, V. & Suresh, M.** 2020. Applications of leagility in manufacturing and service industries. Conference presentation at 5th International conference on Materials and Manufacturing Engineering. Tamilnadu, India, 7-8 September 2020. IOP Publishing. https://iopscience.iop.org/article/10.1088/1757-899X/954/1/012019

322 **Tommasi, F.** 2020 The importance of resilience. An empirical analysis of SMEs in the metropolitan city of Milan. Milan, Italy. University of Milan. Unpublished Doctorate Dissertation https://thesis.unipd.it/handle/20.500.12608/23018?1/Tommasi_Francesco.pdf

323 **Bliss, P.P., Spafford, H.G. & Sims, W.H.** 1982. *It is well with my soul.* Good Life Publications.

324 **Boyd, J.P.** 1942. Horatio Gates Spafford and his historical activities. Conference presentation at Proceedings of the American Antiquarian Society. American Antiquarian Society.

325 **Lewis, D.** 2010. Nongovernmental organizations, definition and history. *International encyclopedia of civil society,* 41(6): 1056-1062. https://doi.org/10.1007/978-0-387-93996-4_3

326 **Adibe, E. & Obiefuna, O.** 2012. Non-Governmental Organisations (NGOs) and global social change-theoretical foundations and practical considerations. *Nnamdi Azikiwe University Journal of International Law and Jurisprudence,* 13(3): 1-14. https://www.ajol.info/index.php/naujilj/article/view/136298

327 **Taliani, J.I.** 2010 Predicting financial distress in commercial banks in Kenya. Kenya. Univesity of Nairobi.

328 **Brown, L.D. & Kalegaonkar, A.** 2002. Support organizations and the evolution of the NGO sector. *Nonprofit and voluntary sector quarterly,* 31(2): 231-258. https://doi.org/10.1177/0899764002312004

329 **Venkatachalam, P., Yeh, D., Rastogi, S., Siddiqui, A., Gupta, K., Shekar, L. & Thompson, R.** 2022. Bridging the gap on funding the true costs of NGOS in India. *Bridgespan Group.* https://www.bridgespan.org

330 **Mhaka-Mutepfa, M. & Maundeni, T.** 2019. The role of faith (spirituality/religion) in resilience in Sub-Saharan African children. *The International Journal of Community and Social Development,* 1(3): 211-233. https://doi.org/10.1177/2516602619859961

331 **Edgerton, G.R., Hart, W.B. & Hassencahl, F.** 2007. Televising 9/11 and its aftermath: The framing of George W. Bush's faith-based politics of good and evil. In: *The changing face of evil in film and television,* pp. 195-214. Brill.

332 **Ogden, E.** Ryder church marks year of drive-in worship services. *Minot Daily News*, April 3, 2021. https://www.minotdailynews.com/news/local-news/2021/04/ryder-church-marks-year-of-drive-in-worship-services/

333 **Waniak-Michalak, H., Leitonienė, Š. & Perica, I.** 2022. The NGOs and Covid 19 pandemic: a new challenge for charitable giving and NGOs' mission models. *Inžinerinė ekonomika*: 174-187. https://doi.org/10.5755/j01.ee.33.2.30005

334 **Hoffmann, R. & Waddington, J.** 2005. *Trade unions in Europe: facing challenges and searching for solutions.* https://www.etui.org

335 **Nissim, G. & Simon, T.** 2021. The future of labor unions in the age of automation and at the dawn of AI. *Technology in Society,* 67. https://doi.org/10.1016/j.techsoc.2021.101732

336 **Al Thobaity, A. & Alshammari, F.** 2020. Nurses on the frontline against the COVID-19 pandemic: an integrative review. *Dubai Medical Journal,* 3(3): 87-92.

337 **Souza, A.C., Alexandre, N.M.C. & Guirardello, E.B.** 2017. Psychometric properties in instruments evaluation of reliability and validity. *Epidemiol Serv Saude,* 26(3): 649-659. https://doi.org/10.5123/S1679-49742017000300022

338 **Alshebami, A.S., Rengarajan, V., Pahlevi, R.W., Said, J. & Sari, W.R.** 2021. Challenges and risk of microfinance sustainability amid Covid-19 pandemic crisis. *Academy of Strategic Management Journal,* 20: 1-5. https://www.abacademies.org/articles/challenges-and-risk-of-microfinance-sustainability-amid-covid19-pandemic-crisis-12807.html

339 **Ali, A. & Khan, A.** 2015. Benefits of community based organizations for community development. *International Journal of Progressive Sciences and Technologies,* 1(2): 39-43. https://doi.org/10.52155/ijpsat.v1.2.15

340 **Smith, R. & Aponte, C.** January 5, 2021. Evolving in COVID Crisis, NYC Mutual Aid Groups head into 2021 with tablets, toys, and diapers. *The City.* https://www.thecity.nyc/life/2021/1/4/22202979/nyc-mutual-aid-groups-covid-head-into-2021-with-expanded-misssion

341 **Water Is Right Foundation**. 2022. *Mathare Youth Environmental Conservation Group at the forefront of Covid-19,* https://www.waterisright.org/kopie-von-mathare-slums

342 **Subathra, G.N., Rajendrababu, S.R., Senthilkumar, V.A., Mani, I. & Udayakumar, B.** 2021. Impact of COVID-19 on follow-up and medication adherence in patients with glaucoma in a tertiary eye care centre in south India. *Indian J Ophthalmol,* 69(5): 1264-1270. https://doi.org/10.4103/ijo.IJO_164_21

343 **FoundationSource**. 2023. *What is private foundation?,* https://foundationsource.com/what-is-a-private-foundation

344 **Dearing, J. & Larson, S.** 2002. Private foundation funding of applied communication research. *Journal of Applied Communication Research,* 30(4): 358-368. https://doi.org/10.1080/00909880216600

345 **Lynn, J., Nolan, C. & Waring, P.** 2021. Strategy resilience: Getting wise about philanthropic strategy in a post-pandemic

world. *The Foundation Review*, 13(2): 8. https://doi. org/10.9707/1944-5660.1564

346 **Zhu, H.-M., Xiao, X.-H. & Tang, Y.** 2022. Creating extraordinary from ordinary: High resource efficiency of underdog entrepreneurs and its mechanism. *Frontiers in Psychology*, 13(851356): 1-17. https://doi.org/10.3389/fpsyg.2022.851356

347 **Schreiber, J.B.** 2021. Issues and recommendations for exploratory factor analysis and principal component analysis. *Res Social Adm Pharm*, 17(5): 1004-1011. https://doi.org/10.1016/j. sapharm.2020.07.027

LIST OF ABBREVIATIONS

Abbreviation	Definition
AIG	American International Group
APSES	Adversity-Practical-Social-Emotional-Spiritual
CBO	Community-Based Organizations
CIGRO	Crisis-Induced Growth Realization Opportunities
CIPMO	Crisis-Induced Profit-Making Opportunities
DCV	Dynamic Capabilities View
DROF	Dynamic Resource Orchestration Framework
FBO	Faith-Based Organizations
FFCRA	Families First Coronavirus Response Act
IsM	Issue Management Scale
LpR	Leadership Personal Resilience
LRI	Leading Resilience Index
MASTER	Management-Strategy-Emergency-Resilience

MECYG	Mathare Environmental Conservation Youth Group
MEN	Male Egoistic Narcissism
MFI	Microfinance institutions
NASA	National Aeronautics and Space Administration
NBMAN	North Brooklyn Mutual Aid Network
NGO	Non-Governmental Organizations
OECD	Organization for Economic Cooperation and Development
PcR	Post-crisis Resilience
PESTEL	Political-Economic-Social-Technological-Environmental-Legal
PrR	Pre-crisis Resilience
PsyCap	Psychological Capital
QaP	Qualitative Assessment Prompts
RlS	Resilience Leadership Strategies
ROV	Resource Orchestration View
RR	Resilience Resource
RrO	Resilience Resource Orchestration
SBA	Small Business Administration
SME	Small and medium-sized enterprises
SOWT	Strengths-Opportunities-Weaknes s-Threats
SpA	Stakeholder Perception Assessment
SWOT	Strengths-Weaknesse s-Opportunities-Threats

VUCA	Volatile, Uncertain, Ambiguous, and Complex
VVT-i	Variable Valve Timing-intelligent
WcR	Within-crisis Resilience
WOMEN	Women's Movement for Emancipation and Normalization

ACKNOWLEDGMENT

Life is a journey and a path. As we journey, we follow a path. Along the journey, we cross, overlap, or maintain parallel paths. Along my own journey, I crossed paths with great leaders who generously passed on their knowledge and contributed to upgrading me into a better version of myself. I want to thank the PAC University faculty. I especially wish to mention Professor Margaret Muthwii, Professor Dionysious Kiambi, Dr. Lilian Vikiru, Dr. James Kilika, Dr. Clare Gakenia, Dr. Truphena Oduol, Dr. Jane Kinuthia, Bishop Emeritus Dr. David Oginde, Dr. Percy Opio, Dr. Edward Nzinga, Dr. Jane Chiroma, Dr. Wilson Odiyo, and Dr. Walter Ongeti.

This work is a culmination of many years of scholarly research and practice. Along the way, I learned, interacted, and collaborated with distinguished colleagues—and admittedly, I cannot find sufficient space to mention them in this book, but I kept ample space for them in my heart and memory. I thank Dr. Solomon Munyao, Dr. Beatrice Oduor, Dr. Daniel Mulinge, Dr. Robert Gitau, Dr. Magdalene Bore, Dr. Thuo Mburu, Dr. Josh Amwago, and Dr. Irungu Macharia.

I thank all those who contributed to refining this book and dressing it elegantly and fashionably. I thank, in particular, Mr. Sylvance Mboha of the Lead Entrepreneurs Network School, who provided high-quality critiquing of the manuscript. I thank Wandering Words Media team for astutely copyediting and proofreading the final text. Beyond their highly professional services, Wandering Words team have been extremely initiative-taking and responsive beyond my expectations. I thank 100-Covers team for elegantly executing a complex yet captivating artwork for the front and cover designs of the book. I thank Formatted Books team for a great and professional layout. I thank Carolyn Weaver of Weaver Indexing Services for professionally indexing the book. A former President of the American Society for Indexing with 32 years in book indexing services, Carolyn has a remarkable history, which she generously brought into this book as evidenced in how this book has been indexed. I thank every person who contributed directly or indirectly to making this book a reality. I thank my family for their support.

ABOUT THE AUTHOR

Eltigani Ahmed holds a Doctor of Philosophy (Ph.D.) in organizational leadership—Business and Enterpreneurship and a Master of Philosophy (M.Phil) in Economics and Finance. He has over two decades of international banking experience and, in those years, led dozens of teams in creating impactful projects, facilitating multibillion-dollar deals, and growing businesses across Africa. Dr. Ahmed's interest in organizational resilience, leadership strategy, resource orchestration, and firm resource management led to a myriad of career successes as well as several publications, including groundbreaking publications in Inderscience's *International Journal of Business and Emerging Markets, International Journal of Finance & Banking Studies, International Journal of Organizational Leadership, and International Journal of Business Ecosystem & Strategy* (among others). He is also credited for jointly proposing resource orchestration measurement inventory with Dr. James Kilika of Kenyatta University and Dr. Clare Gakenia of United States International University. Dr. Ahmed currently leads Trade Finance Operations in one of the highest-rated Multilateral Development Banks covering 44 African countries. Besides his professional and writing activities, Dr. Ahmed loves discovering unfamiliar places and making new connections. He lives in Nairobi with his family. You can find out more about Dr. Ahmed and his projects here: [https://arcoired.org].

AUTHOR PUBLICATIONS

Published Works

2021   An empirical assessment of the adoption and innovation of portable banking technology
Indian Journal of Finance and Banking

2021   Leadership and organizational distress: a review of the literature
International Journal of Research in Business and Social Science

2021   Progressive convergent definition and conceptualization of organizational resilience: A model development
International Journal of Organizational Leadership

2021   SME resilience to COVID-19: Insights from nonessential service providers
International Journal of Finance & Banking Studies

2021   The conceptualization of DROF as an anchor for organizational resilience
International Journal of Research in Business and Social Science

2022   Strategy-induced organizational resilience through dynamic resource orchestration
International Journal of Research in Business and Social Science

2022   Organizational transformation through resilience leadership strategy
International Journal of Finance & Banking Studies

2022	Definition, operationalization, and measurement of resilience leadership strategy *International Journal of Organizational Leadership*
2023	Development of an inventory for the resource orchestration construct *Inderscience Journal of Business and Emerging Markets*

Work in Progress

2023	Ukraine resilience: intangible resource differential approach
2023	Development of a theory for organizational resilience constants
2023	Practical insights on the construction and empirical application of mixed methods research design
2023	The impact of systemic disruptive shocks on banking resilience

INDEX